WITHDRAWN

GREAT BUSINESS STORIES

GEORGE EASTMAN AND KODAK

PETER BROOKE-BALL

OTHER TITLES IN THE SERIES
Akio Morita and Sony by David Marshall
Anita Roddick and The Body Shop by Paul Brown
Bill Gates and Microsoft by David Marshall
Coco Chanel and Chanel by David Bond
Henry Ford and Ford by Michael Pollard

Picture Credits
The Advertising Archives: 34, 35 (top left); **AKG:** 28 (top); **Allsport UK Ltd:** 20-21 (both)/John Gichigi, 58-59/Gray Mortimore; **Ann Ronan:** 18, 22 (both), 29 (top), 35 (top right and bottom), 38 (bottom); **J. L. Charmet:** 12; **Edimedia:** 28 (bottom)/Coll Kharbine; **Gamma:** 5/Ferry-Liaison, 30 (top), 32-33 (main pic)/Phil Matt, 55 (top)/Eric Bouvet, 59 (top)/G. Merillon, (bottom)/Gilles Saussier; **George Eastman House:** 42/Joseph Dinunzio; **Image Select:** 36 (bottom), 45, 47, 50-51 (all); **The Kobal Collection:** 46; **Kodak Limited:** 30 (bottom), 33 (inset, both), 54, 56 (all), 57, 60/Jim McGuckin; **The National Museum of Photography, Film and Television:** 7 (top), 9 (bottom), 13, 25 (bottom), 27, 38 (top), 48 (bottom); **NMPFT/Science and Society Picture Library:** 10; **Popperfoto:** 26; Range/Bettmann: 9 (top), 48 (top), 49; **Rex Features:** 4/Henryk T. Kaiser, 19, 44; **Royal Photographic Society:** cover, 6/Cuthbert Bede, 7 (bottom)/L. Tisserand, 11, 15, 23, 24, 29 (bottom), 31, 36 (top), 37 (bottom), 39, 40 (all), Baron De Meyer (bottom right only); **The Science Museum:** 8, 25 (top), 37 (top).

Published in Great Britain in 1994
by Exley Publications Ltd,
16 Chalk Hill, Watford,
Herts WD1 4BN, United Kingdom.

Copyright © Exley Publications, 1994
Copyright © Peter Brooke-Ball, 1994

A copy of the CIP data is available from the British Library on request.

ISBN 1-85015-492-9

All rights reserved. No part of this publication may be reproduced or transmitted in any form or by any means, electronic or mechanical, including photocopy, recording or any information storage and retrieval system without permission in writing from the Publisher.

Series editor: Samantha Armstrong
Editorial assistants: Helen Lanz and Alison MacTier
Picture editors: Alex and Dora Goldberg of Image Select
Typeset by Delta Print, Watford, Herts, U.K.
Printed in Hungary

GEORGE EASTMAN
AND
KODAK

PETER BROOKE-BALL

🇸 EXLEY

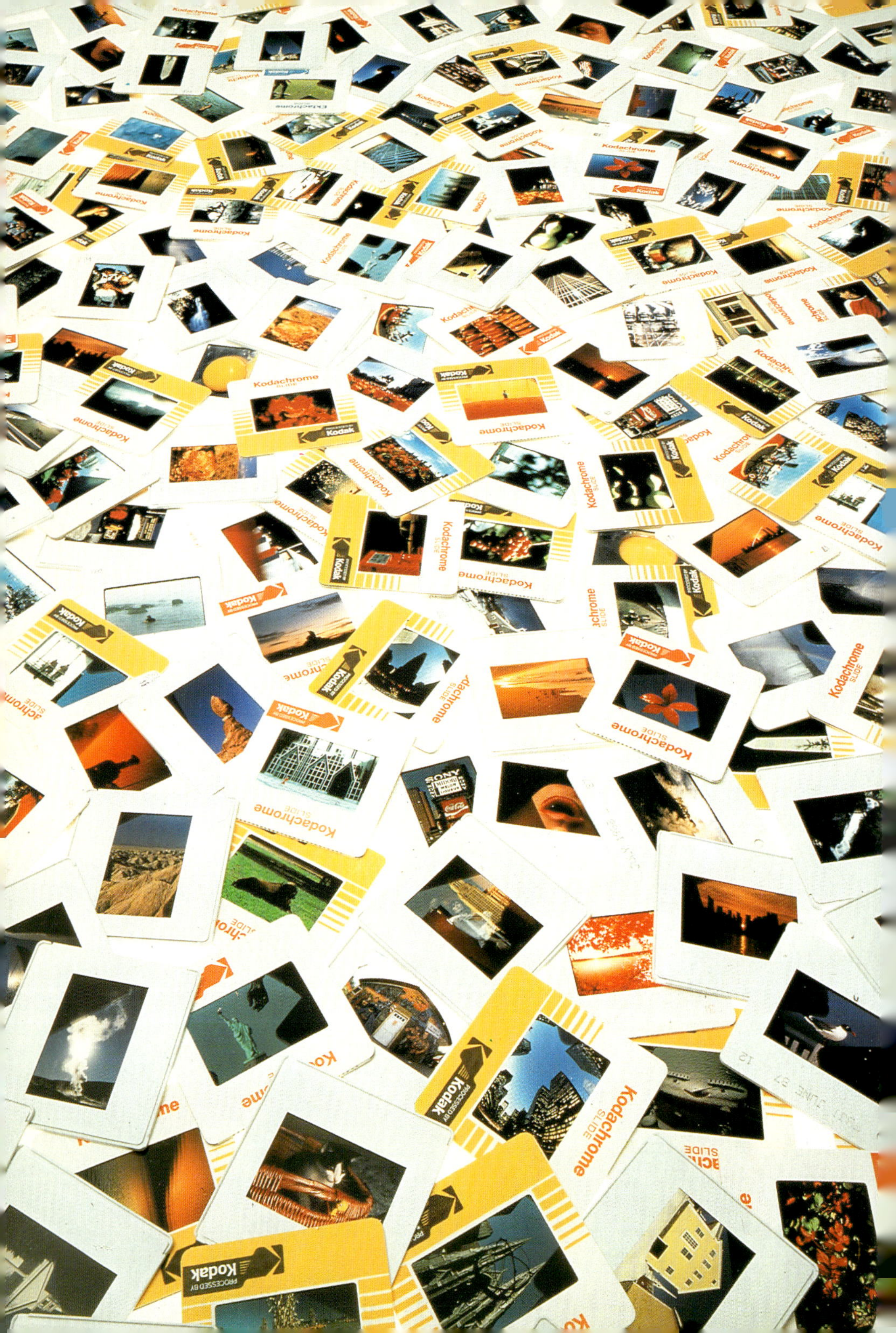
Kodachrome
SLIDE
PROCESSED BY
Kodak
Ektachrome

"Everybody can use it"

Kodak is one of the most famous brand names in the world and to most people, regardless of language, it represents just one thing – photography. The man who created the company and simplified the complicated process of photography was George Eastman.

George Eastman took up photography as a hobby when he was twenty-four – it was a relatively new art form enjoyed only by an elite. He quickly spotted its potential and resolved "to make the camera as convenient as the pencil."

Eastman discovered an interest that was ripe for development and with his tirelessly inventive mind and acute business sense he succeeded where others with similar ambitions failed. Within the span of just twenty years, he and his company made photography available and accessible to millions.

As his company grew, Eastman became a wealthy and powerful man, but he was never a conventional businessman. He shunned personal publicity. He was shrewd and wily in business affairs, but he looked

Above: You can even use a Kodak upside down in a war zone! Opposite: Kodak introduced the world's first slide film, Kodachrome, in 1935. Millions of rolls of Kodak's modern Kodachrome and Ektachrome films are sold every year.

"Kodak's aim is to be the best in the world at what we do – to set the standards that others have to follow."

From **Kodak in the U.K.**, a Kodak publication.

A pen-and-ink caricature ridiculing a photographer as he carries his heavy burden under the beaming sun. Dating from the second half of the century, this cartoon and many like it, took delight in mocking the cumbersome nature of photography – something that George Eastman was determined to rectify.

after his work force as if it were extended family. Perhaps one of the most surprising things of all was that Eastman gave the bulk of his fortune away.

By the 1990s, Kodak had become one of the twenty-five largest businesses in the United States. Its interests had spread far and wide beyond the confines of photography – it manufactured pharmaceuticals, textiles, and electronic goods. It had come a long way from its modest start in a rented warehouse attic.

A hobby

After working for four solid years as a bank clerk, twenty-four year old George Eastman decided that he deserved a break. Santo Domingo in the Caribbean island of Hispaniola seemed to be just the right place – a place as different as possible from Rochester, New York, his home town on the southern shore of Lake Ontario in the United States.

Getting to the island of Hispaniola, however, posed a few problems. The year was 1878 and long-distance travel was expensive, slow, and potentially dangerous. These factors were not enough to prevent George Eastman from planning his long-awaited trip.

He discussed his hopes and fears with work colleagues and one friend suggested that he take a camera with him, saying that if any of the pictures were good, he might be able to sell them when he got back. Eastman knew that this was going to be an amazing experience and that his friend was right – the journey would be worth recording. He spent a whole month's salary on a photographic kit, little knowing where that one purchase would lead him.

A change of heart

Eastman described what he got for his money as "a packhorse load" of equipment – and his kit only contained the basic essentials. It included a black developing tent, developing trays, assorted bottles of chemicals, and large jugs for water. The camera itself was a large wooden box.

Above: Roger Fenton's photographic van. In the 1860s and 1870s, Fenton and photographers like him hawked their trade around the United States in horse-drawn carts.

Left: A photographer readies the camera as his assistant stands by with a prepared wet plate.

Cameras from the mid-1800s. The Dark Brown (left) and miniature Mousetrap cameras had similar designs – a lens projected an image onto a photographic plate inserted at the back. The camera obscura (right) was not used to take photographs – it projected an inverted image onto a glass screen.

Opposite top: George Eastman sat for this wet plate portrait when he was thirteen. He had recently lost his father and was about to take a job as a messenger boy to support the family.

But this was by no means all that a photographer of the time had to carry. A sturdy tripod held the camera perfectly still for the ten to forty seconds that it took to take the picture. The photographic images were made on heavy, fragile glass plates which were inserted into the back of the camera. These plates had to be coated with photographic emulsion just before each picture was taken. This emulsion was wet, so the process was called "wet-plate" photography. All the preparation of the plates and subsequent developing had to be carried out in total darkness – and quickly. Overall it took more than twenty minutes to take one photograph. Undeterred by all the paraphernalia, George Eastman decided to take lessons in how to take photographs.

Despite all the cumbersome gear and the disappointments of the hit-and-miss techniques that were standard at the time, Eastman found himself increasingly absorbed by the process of photography. The more photographs he took, the more he wanted to learn. Slowly the pull of Hispaniola gave way to the even greater lure of the camera and the trip was put off. But, he remembered, "That did not matter so much because, in making ready, I had become wholly absorbed by photography."

Eastman became quite expert at taking photographs but proudly insisted on calling himself an amateur, wanting the word to be interpreted literally – "one who carries out his art for the love of it." He loved all the chemical processes involved and had the persistence of a true inventor.

Inventor

Although George Eastman was captivated by the processes of photography, he gradually became more and more frustrated by them. Not only were the procedures complicated and difficult to carry out, but there was so much that could go wrong at each stage. He decided to look into ways of simplifying the steps – starting with the messy and precarious business of preparing the photographic plates.

Although he had no training in chemistry, George Eastman pored over journals and books looking for possible changes to the processes. He even taught himself basic French and German so that he could read international photography magazines.

One evening, while flipping through a British photography article, he recognized a solution to his problem. A few dedicated photographers on the other side of the Atlantic were experimenting with different kinds of emulsion. Plates coated with these new home-made emulsions remained sensitive to light for months after they were dry. This meant that the troublesome wet plates could be things of the past. Too impatient to wait for others to perfect these new emulsions, Eastman immediately began concocting his own versions in his mother's kitchen.

Inventor turned entrepreneur

It did not take Eastman long to realize that if he could perfect the recipe, he could make photographic plates, not just for himself, but for others as well – he could go into business.

Above: The camera used by Louis Daguerre.

Opposite: An 1884 portrait of George Eastman. This was one of the first photographs to be taken on American film.

Above: A tintype portrait of George Eastman at the age of three in 1857. Tintypes were made by coating metal with photographic emulsion and were often used by commercial photographers.

With fiery determination, George Eastman worked in the bank during the day and turned his mother's kitchen into an improvised laboratory at night. To her despair, he frequently became so worn out with his experiments that he fell asleep, fully clothed, beside the kitchen stove.

He was a perfectionist and was not dismayed by his frequent failures – if anything, these spurred him on. Gradually he got closer to his goal. It took him two years to formulate an emulsion recipe with which he was truly happy. He was then twenty-six, and that emulsion was to become the foundation of one of the most powerful and influential companies in the world, the Eastman Kodak Company.

A tough beginning

George Eastman was born on July 12, 1854 to relatively wealthy parents, George Washington and Maria Kilbourn Eastman. His father ran a nursery business in the small town of Waterville, in upstate New York, and earned more than enough to support the family of three children – baby George and his two elder sisters, Ellen and Emma.

George Sr. was ambitious and when his son was six, he moved the family to the flourishing town of Rochester to establish a business school named the Eastman Commercial College. At first the college was a success, but just two years after arriving in Rochester, George Sr. died suddenly. Without its founder, the college began to fail. In a short time, the once prosperous Eastman family was left almost penniless.

Maria Eastman was very resourceful, however, and used her one remaining asset, the family home, and took in lodgers. By saving what little she had, Maria managed to keep her family together.

George's school career was unremarkable. He was meticulous in his work, but was not academically brilliant. He enjoyed playing baseball and having fun.

Perhaps George was not in school long enough for his talents to show through – he left when he was just fourteen. One of his sisters contracted polio and was disabled. Shouldering responsibility for the

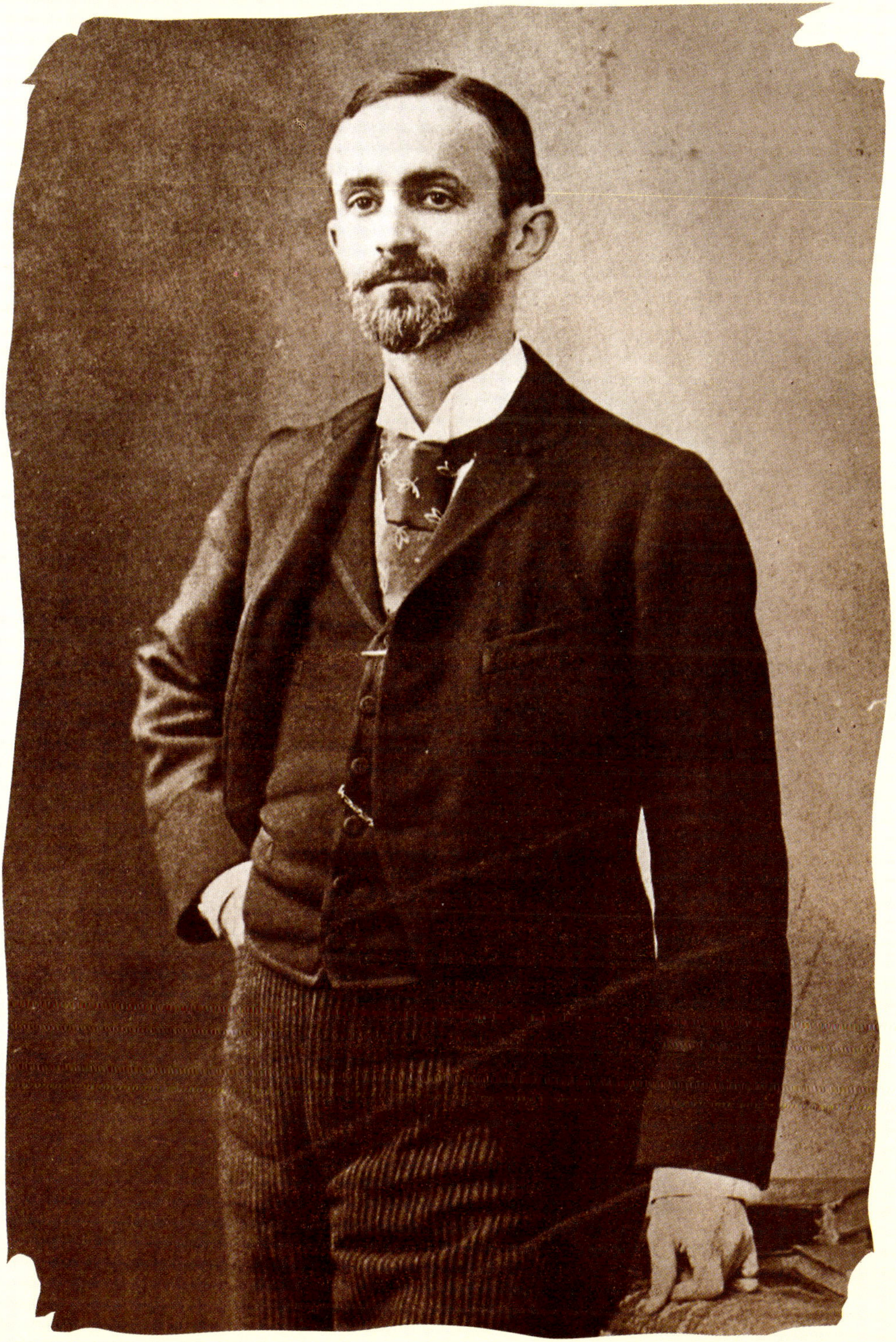

A daguerrotype photograph. Family portraits were often the subject matter of early photographs. The quality was poor but the image clear enough to be kept as a keepsake. Eastman Kodak expanded the world of photography far beyond these images into space photography and medical uses.

family, George took a job as an insurance messenger boy. At fifteen, he moved to another insurance company and worked his way up to become a $5 a week filing clerk. George knew that salary was never going to be enough to provide adequately for the family, and he could see that he was never going to get a better job without qualifications. So he started to study accountancy in the evenings. In 1874, at the age of twenty, he was taken on as a junior clerk at the Rochester Savings Bank.

George Eastman's dedication to his day job at the bank stemmed from his early life when money in the family was short. His motivation was founded on need, not greed. Throughout his life George Eastman was generous with his money to those who needed it. He was not, however, one to fritter money away – even when he was first earning he saved a few cents out of each pay packet. By the time he was planning his trip to Hispaniola, he had saved $3,000.

The first photographers

When Eastman first stumbled into photography in 1878, it was still very much in its infancy and had not advanced very far since its invention in 1826.

A French chemist, Joseph Niepce, is credited with taking the very first photograph – a faint image on a metal plate. Niepce teamed up with another Frenchman, the painter Louis Daguerre, and together they perfected what became known as the daguerreotype – a type of photograph made on copper sheets coated with iodized silver. The first daguerreotype was made in 1839 and, in the same year, an Englishman named William Fox Talbot made what he called a "photographic drawing" on silver chloride paper. Two years later, Fox Talbot invented the first negative from which prints could be made.

Photography was largely in the hands of those who were wealthy enough to finance their own experiments. Progress was sluggish and the next step forward did not come until 1851 when Englishman, Frederick Scott Archer invented the wet plate process with which George Eastman became so familiar. Cumbersome though it was, wet-plate photography

William Fox Talbot's camera which he experimented with in 1839. Talbot's very first "photographic drawing" – the faint image of a lattice window – is shown in the background.

was relatively reliable and enabled photographers to predict results with some degree of accuracy.

A dry plate was invented by R. L. Maddox in 1871, some seven years before George Eastman became interested in photography. But only a few people were either willing or able to take up the challenge of pushing forward the development of the dry plate. Perhaps the majority of photographers were not convinced that it had any future or felt that the wet-plate system seemed adequate. As a result, dry-plate photography was largely ignored – only a few photographers were prepared to gamble with the new process as the majority of pictures came out a heart-rending black. George Eastman was one of them.

The value of patents

Soon after Eastman started dabbling in photography, he came up with a satisfactory emulsion recipe for dry-plate photography. He was convinced that he could go into business selling dry plates, but he also acknowledged that there was more to making a successful business than a good idea.

"George Eastman's inventive genius revolutionized photography. When he began as an amateur to take pictures, the technique of photography was difficult and the apparatus cumbersome. He made photographers of the world's people by simplifying the entire process."

From George Eastman, *a Kodak publication.*

13

One problem the twenty-six year old had to overcome was the way in which he coated the plates with the emulsion. So far, he had simply brushed it on by hand – a slow process that would be impossible to sustain if the business were to grow and succeed. To overcome this, Eastman indulged his creativity and determination again and constructed a machine to coat the plates. Mass production of uniform and reliable products was, he could see, the key to success in business.

Once the demand for dry plates increased, other photographic product manufacturers would need a machine to coat them. It followed that since Eastman had just invented such a machine, it would be worthwhile to patent its design. This would give him ownership and the sole right to make, use, and sell the design. Anyone who wanted to copy Eastman's machine would have to pay him a fee. In 1879, George Eastman took some money out of his savings and went by ship to England where most of the advances in photography were being made. Patents have to be taken out in each individual country and eventually the patent for Eastman's emulsion-coating machine was granted in London. When he returned to the United States, Eastman also took out a U.S. patent for the machine. His foresight was perfect.

In October 1879, the British photographic company Mawson & Swan bought the right to manufacture and use George Eastman's dry-plate coating machine.

Open for business

Another problem that worried Eastman was financing his business. Although he had almost $3,000 in his savings, he knew that he would need more to establish a business. He would have to buy equipment and materials, rent factory space, and pay wages, before he could expect any returns on sales. He wrote to his Uncle Horace to ask for a loan, but the conservative Uncle Horace thought the venture was far too risky and rejected his nephew's plea to support his business plan.

"[Eastman] did these things that he believed in with a spirit of amateur devotion for the love of doing them well."

From George Eastman, *a Kodak publication.*

Disappointed by his uncle's refusal to help, Eastman decided to go into business anyway, his own savings boosted by the cash from Mawson & Swan. In 1880, Eastman started to produce photographic dry plates on a commercial basis from a rented attic in Rochester. To his surprise and relief, financial help did come, although it was from an unexpected quarter. One of his mother's former lodgers, Henry Strong, was successfully making whips for horse-drawn buggies, the transportation of the day. Strong knew little about photography, but he too was a wily businessman. He decided to invest in Eastman's budding company in 1880 and then again in 1881, when it officially became the Eastman Dry Plate Company. The money was used to buy equipment, pay wages, and rent new premises. In exchange, Strong expected to take a share of the company's profits in proportion to the amount of money he had invested. However, if the business failed, then Strong stood to lose his money. As well as being an investor, Strong also became a partner and joint owner of the company. As partners, Eastman and Strong were responsible for running the company and making business decisions.

As in all successful partnerships, the two men trusted each other – Eastman valued Strong's understanding of business issues and Strong had absolute faith in Eastman's ambitions and his acquired knowledge of photography.

Below: A box of Eastman's revolutionary dry plates which were first manufactured on a commercial basis in 1880. This product represented the beginning of Kodak's reputation for creating innovative products for photographers and marked a change in the course of photography.

Faulty products

When the Eastman Dry Plate Company moved to the third floor of a warehouse in Rochester, twenty-seven year old Eastman still worked at the bank during the day and cooked up emulsions during the evening. He only had one helper to assist in the running of the business.

However, that soon changed as sales began to pick up. There were still relatively few people who took photographs, but those who did were enthusiastic

"My desires are only limited by my imagination."
George Eastman, 1896.

George Eastman as the debonair businessman. A formal portrait of George Eastman in his thirties.

and invariably discussed the new inventions that were coming onto the market. The word on Eastman's dry plates was good – both amateurs and professionals praised their quality. The *Philadelphia Photographer* magazine said, "The plates . . . negatives of both summer and winter scenes were characterized by a great delicacy of detail in either light or shadows. This I considered a most difficult test."

The increase in sales was so great that after just a year, the company had moved to larger premises three times. Eastman continued to work by day at the bank until September 1881, by which time the company was turning over $4,000 a month.

The Eastman Dry Plate Company appeared to be running perfectly until 1882. Then suddenly people began to return the plates saying they were useless. When he examined the plates, Eastman had to agree and he immediately began looking for the cause of the problem. By March, he had personally completed some five hundred experiments in trying to find the fault with no success. After a hasty trip to Mawson & Swan in England, it was discovered that the fault lay not in the photographic emulsion but in impurities in the gelatin that was used.

At considerable cost, Eastman replaced all the defective plates with new ones. "Making good on those plates took our last dollar," George Eastman recalled. "But what we had left was more important – reputation." To Eastman, replacing the faulty plates was a natural thing to do, but other companies might not have been so eager to compensate their customers. His simple gesture did much to boost the image of the company.

By the end of that same year, 1882, the company had made so many sales that it could afford to build a new factory and still have money left over after all expenses and wages had been paid. It was a formidable achievement to make a profit after a year in which the company had been brought to the brink of collapse.

Marketing photography

The year following the near-catastrophe, Eastman and Strong moved their company to yet another new building – an even bigger factory. By any standard, the growth of the company had been extraordinary. Its success had been founded on a new product of consistent quality and fair trading – two principles that encouraged photographers to buy Eastman's products rather than anybody else's. George Eastman, with his shrewd vision for the future, was eager to continue to build on that.

However, the number of people who took photographs remained a tiny proportion of the population as a whole – despite the introduction of the dry plate. The art of photography was a complicated business and most people were wary of it. All the photographic suppliers in the United States seemed happy with the current situation. They marketed what was made by a host of small

"The ideal large corporation is the one that makes the best use of the brains within it."

George Eastman.

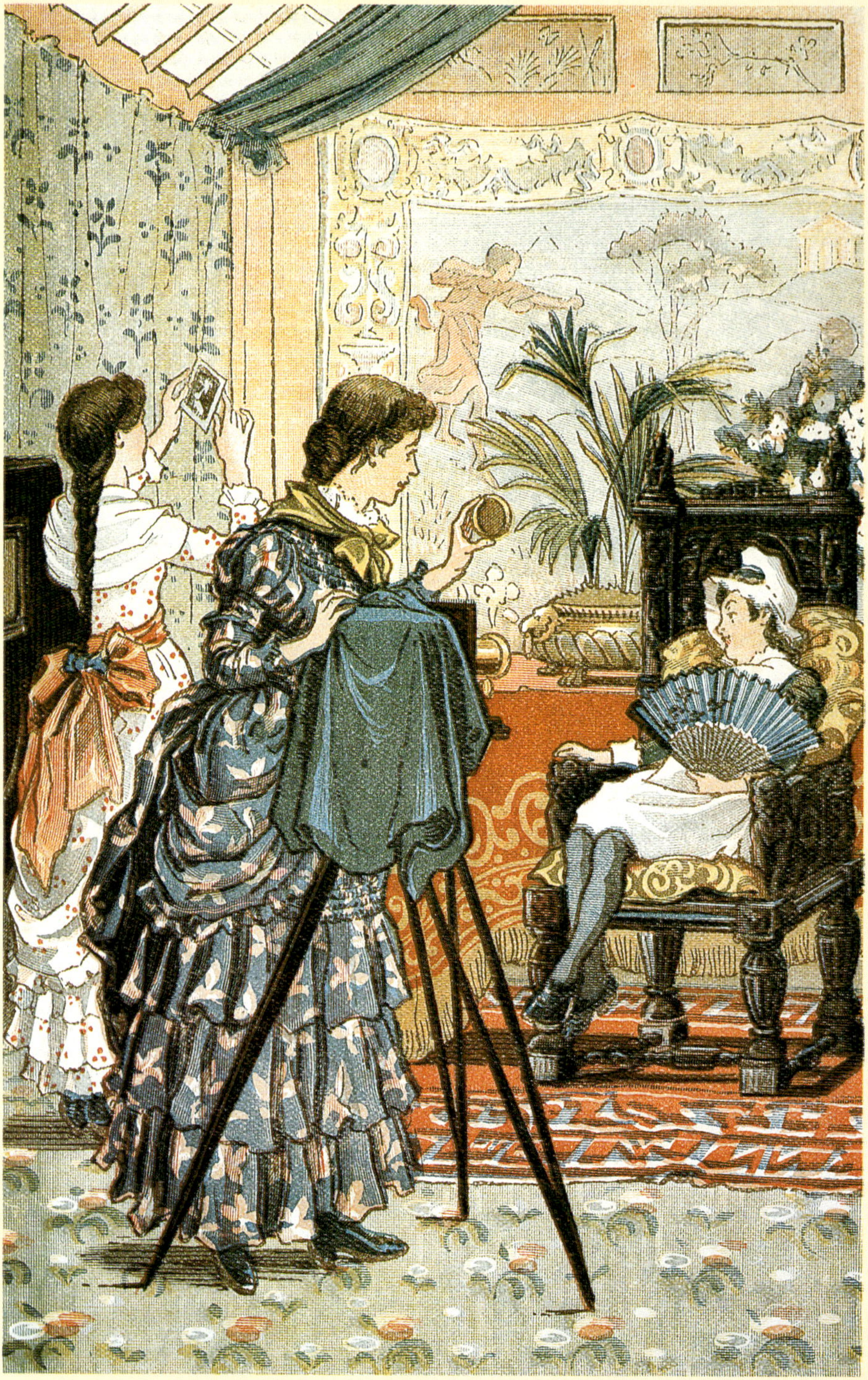

companies to established photographers; they did not seem to be concerned about making more people interested in photography and thereby increasing sales. To the ambitious Eastman, who wanted to see his business get even bigger, this seemed a waste of business potential and he sought out ways to make photography less exclusive.

He drafted four simple business guidelines that he believed were crucial for success: Mass-produce goods using machines. Keep prices low. Distribute goods nationally and internationally. Advertise and sell products by demonstration.

To Eastman, these four ideas were linked together – if a product was mass-produced it could be sold cheaply, but, in order to sell it, people had to be made aware of the product by advertising. He also felt that there was little point in limiting himself to the United States market – why not export as well? However, in order to make his business plans work, Eastman knew that he had to persuade people that photography was not as difficult as it seemed and he had to have a product that many people would want to buy.

Inventing film

To make photography universally popular, Eastman knew that photographic equipment would have to be simplified – the average person did not take readily to handling glass plates, heavy cameras, and all the other equipment. He decided that the next place to start changing things was with the glass plates themselves.

Eastman felt that paper could be an effective support for a photographic emulsion instead of the heavy glass plates. In many ways paper seemed ideal – it was inexpensive and flexible. So Eastman began to experiment once more and made an emulsion that could satisfactorily be mounted on paper as thin as film.

Paper, however, did not let light through so any print made from a paper-based negative was always blurred. To make the paper transparent it was brushed with a special castor oil-based liquid called

Opposite: A romantic view of photography seen through the eyes of an illustrator of the late nineteenth century. The woman in the middle is pictured removing the lens cap, while counting out seconds, to expose the wet plate at the back of the camera.

Below: An early portrait photographer keeps an eye on the time as he holds the camera shutter open. Meanwhile, his customer tries hard not to blink.

> "No one could come in contact with him [Eastman] without realizing that he possessed a remarkable mind, shrewd, keen, penetrating, capable of making quick decisions and standing by them resolutely."
>
> From the Rochester Democrat and Chronicle.

Modern technology allows rolls of exposed film to be developed automatically in machines. Here a technician removes strips of film from developer and is about to hang them up to dry.

Translucene. The new product had only limited success, but Eastman considered it to be worth marketing. He was also sufficiently confident in the future of film (the word just referred to the thin emulsion coating rather than the paper support) that he changed the name of the company to the Eastman Dry Plate and Film Company.

In 1884, Eastman placed an advertisement in leading photography magazines to promote the company and its new product: "Shortly after January 1, 1885, the Eastman Dry Plate and Film Company will introduce a new sensitive film which it is believed will prove an economical and convenient substitute for glass dry plates both for outdoor and studio work."

There was more to the new name than was immediately obvious. The company was no longer a simple partnership between Eastman and Strong – it now had fourteen other people who had invested money in it and stood to lose or gain depending on how the company did.

Henry Strong was made president – in theory, this made him head of the company, although he actually had little to do with the day-to-day running of the business. At the same time, Eastman became treasurer and general manager. As treasurer, Eastman's task was to monitor the financial state of the company, and as general manager, he took care of running the organization.

Room for improvement

Eastman's new film, which was manufactured in long strips, was placed on the market with a special roll holder. This holder, which enabled a roll of paper negatives to be wound from one spool onto another, had been devised, in conjunction with Eastman, by a camera maker named William Walker.

It was made in a variety of sizes to suit different cameras and was specifically designed to replace traditional glass plate holders. Each roll of film could have anything up to twenty-four exposures – this meant that the photographer no longer had to carry a box of twenty-four heavy glass plates!

The roller and the paper film, both of which had been patented as was Eastman's custom, were revolutionary. But not everybody saw them as such and few people were prepared to buy them. "When we started with our scheme of film photography we expected that everybody who used glass plates would take up films, but we found that the number who did so was relatively small and in order to make a large business we would have to reach the general public," George remembered.

Paper film did not catch on; most photographers preferred to stick with the dry plates that gave excellent quality prints and the general public was still reluctant to take up photography as a hobby.

Try and try again

Eastman was not deterred by the apparent failure of his invention. By the end of 1885, he was manufacturing what he called American film. This had three layers: a paper support, a layer of water-soluble gelatin, and a top layer of photographic emulsion. After the film had been exposed, the middle layer was melted by pouring water over the top. The photographic emulsion was then stripped off and strengthened by being coated with another layer of gelatin. This strip was then dried and could be used for making prints. Before marketing the American film, Eastman took the precaution of taking out patents not only on the product, but on the preparation processes as well.

The quality of American film negatives was excellent, but the developing procedure was very complicated and daunting. Although the product sold in reasonable quantities, it failed to secure Eastman the huge new market that he knew was beckoning.

Making the most of equipment

Always quick to learn from an apparently failed venture, George Eastman adapted the film-making equipment that had been installed in the factory to make a different type of paper – bromide paper.

Once developed and dry, the negative film is used to create positive prints. The final stage is to cut the film into convenient strips ready for packaging and then to mount them in cardboard cases.

The English photographer Fox Talbot was the first person to invent the negative (bottom) from which any number of positive prints (top) can be made. Eastman recognized the potential of this idea and his company started to produce the first negative film in 1884.

Negatives could be printed onto bromide paper, but the images could only be developed using chemicals in a darkroom. Bromide had always been largely ignored because it was messy and awkward. Silver chloride paper, which was clamped tight to a negative and left in the sun until a positive image appeared, was normally used.

Bromide paper, however, was soon to become the standard printing paper. One of its great advantages was that it could be used for making enlargements. Seeing the potential in this, Eastman started to offer an enlargement service – photographers could send negatives to the company and have prints made measuring anything up to 30 x 25 inches (76 x 63cm). This broke new ground. Until Eastman established this service, all photographers did their own developing and printing.

It was during 1886 that Eastman, perhaps reluctantly, realized that his films were not going to revolutionize photography after all. He also began to accept his own limitations as a chemist. He had not been trained as a chemist at all, he was merely a self-taught, but extremely successful, amateur. The development of the product he craved was beyond his scope so he hired a research chemist, Henry Reichenbach. The newcomer was immediately given two tasks: first, to develop photographic emulsions so that they became faster and more sensitive and second, to create a strong, flexible, transparent base on which the emulsions could be coated.

Another try

In the spring of 1887, Eastman turned his attention to manufacturing cameras. The first cameras produced by his company were simple dry-plate cameras, but he was really more interested in developing a successful "detective" camera. These cameras were so called because they were tiny in comparison with the bulky, large format cameras that most photographers used. Eastman reasoned that the average person would be more attracted to a small camera than a big one. He also wanted to make a camera that would use film and therefore be easy to operate.

Unfortunately, the product was a dismal failure – just fifty were produced and few of these were actually sold. Though he was bitterly disappointed, George Eastman refused to give up. He remained convinced that his basic idea of a compact, simple camera was right.

What does it mean?

A new word came into being in June 1888. At first it had people puzzled – some thought it came from an obscure foreign language, while others just thought it was a meaningless joke. Before long, however, the word would be spoken throughout the world and everyone would know what it meant. George Eastman dreamt up the word Kodak to describe a new compact camera he had designed. For some time he had been searching for a strong, punchy word that would be difficult to forget. When he hit on Kodak, he was quick to register it as a trademark – he knew he had conjured up the perfect word for his new product.

Eastman was quizzed as to the meaning of the strange word.

The original Kodak camera, first marketed in 1888. It realized Eastman's dream of manufacturing a simple, reliable camera that even a child could use.

"I devised the name myself," he revealed. "The letter 'K' had been a favorite with me – it seems a strong, incisive sort of letter. It became a question of trying out a great number of combinations of letters that made words starting and ending with a 'k'." In

> *"The Kodak camera created an entirely new market and made photographers of people who had no special knowledge of the subject and who had as their only qualification the desire to take pictures."*
>
> From George Eastman, a Kodak publication.

Opposite: Publicity posters of the early 1900s. For years photography had been the almost exclusive preserve of men. Eastman was anxious to make it available to women and children and incorporated women holding cameras into Kodak advertisements.

Below: An 1895 lapel badge. The camera's design, coupled with publicity, made Kodak familiar to millions.

Eastman's application for a trademark, he wrote down the following by way of explanation: "Kodak – This is not a foreign name or word; it was constructed by me to serve a definite purpose. It has the following merits as a trademark word. First: It is short. Second: It is not capable of mispronunciation. Third: It does not resemble anything in the art and cannot be associated with anything in the art except the Kodak."

The new Kodak camera was light, compact, and almost foolproof. The camera did not even have a viewfinder – all the photographer had to do was simply aim a "V" embossed on the top of the casing at the subject. It came loaded with enough American film to take one hundred photographs and the photographer pulled a cord to prepare the shutter, wound on the film, and pressed the button – George Eastman had successfully reduced photography to just three steps!

Careful expansion

Besides the camera itself, the purchaser also got a tiny notebook to record the details of each picture taken and an explanatory booklet, written by Eastman himself, called the *Kodak Primer*.

The Kodak camera's design was brilliant, but that was not all that made it a huge success.

Knowing that the public at large was scared of photography and all the messy chemicals that were associated with it, Eastman decided that the company should do all the tricky developing.

When the film was finished, the photographer sent the camera back to the factory, where, for a small fee, the film was developed and printed and the camera was loaded with fresh film. The final brilliance was the slogan used to sell the Kodak. It was simple and said it all: "You press the button – We do the rest." Determined to capture the interest of those who had never taken a photograph before, Eastman advertised the camera not just in photography magazines, but also in the popular press. Similarly, the camera could be bought from pharmacies and general stores, and not just from photography stores.

Take a KODAK with you
and win the £1000 Daily Mail prize for the best holiday

Advertising

Eastman was quick to become aware of the power of advertising. Promoting products was not a new idea, but Eastman was one of the first entrepreneurs to analyze it and to set aside a fixed amount of money for advertising.

To convey what he considered to be the universal acceptability of his products, Eastman came up with the concept of the "Kodak Girl." In a short time, this image of a beautiful and smiling woman became something of an icon. She was always happy and surrounded by friends and always carrying a Kodak camera. As Eastman intended, she particularly appealed to teenagers who were the very people he wanted to start buying his products. Her picture of youthful freedom was placed in magazines, newspapers, and on billboards. She became known internationally; in Britain she was dubbed the Blue Girl and in France, Dame Kodak.

Now is the time to get your KODAK

> "The films have ... passed through the tropics, through one Antarctic winter buried in the snow, and have lain through another winter in the temperature which must have fallen eighty degrees below zero, before development and after exposure.... They must beyond all question be the most remarkable negatives in the world."
>
> H. G. Ponting, photographer on Captain Scott's expedition to the South Pole, praising Kodak film in a letter to Eastman, 1913.

Robert Peary captured on Kodak film in 1909. Testimonials conveyed the reliability of Kodak products to the general public.

In her various guises, the Kodak Girl was used to promote Kodak products for decades – Eastman believed that to push home the name of Kodak, a consistently recognizable image was essential. However, Eastman did not stick with just one idea to sell his cameras and films. Far from it – he was perpetually seeking innovative techniques. One of his most successful ploys was to exploit testimonials from famous people. He particularly liked what explorers had to say about his films and cameras. He was delighted when the first man to reach the North Pole, Robert Peary, preferred Kodak products and he let the world know about it. Eastman also used one of the first electric billboards in England's capital city – London. He wooed the public with a huge electric billboard that flashed the single word "Kodak." There was no need to explain who or what Kodak was – everybody already knew.

Success

The Kodak camera became such a success that the word "Kodak" became the same as saying "camera"; people would say "Bring your Kodak" instead of "Bring your camera." The slogan entered everyday speech: politicians and comedians tried their best to incorporate "You press the button – We do the rest" into speeches and performances.

In 1888, less than a year after its creation, thirteen thousand Kodak cameras were sold – most camera manufacturers counted sales in tens rather than hundreds. It was all made possible thanks to Eastman's visionary strategy of producing large quantities cheaply, using machinery rather than traditional craft workers. His intention had been to produce a "complete system of practical photography," and in this he was entirely successful. His plan had been to demystify photography and make it available to everyone.

Eastman's forward-thinking philosophy did not please everybody. Die-hard amateurs who enjoyed painstakingly developing snapshots considered the Kodak an intrusion. Their moans were hardly heard, though, amid the excitement of the general public.

The Reverend Hannibal

For some two years the research chemist, Henry Reichenbach, had been struggling to formulate a strong, transparent base for photographic emulsion. Success finally came late in 1888 when he concocted a transparent film that was both clear and strong.

A delighted Reichenbach hurried to perfect the manufacturing process so that it could be patented. However, to his surprise, the patent office said that a similar formula had been presented some twelve years earlier by an amateur photographer named Reverend Hannibal Goodwin.

A legal argument over who had perfected the formula raged on and off for the next twenty-five years. Kodak did get its patent on the process, but this would not be the last time that Kodak would get embroiled in costly legal disputes.

Eastman had anticipated that the new film would be a success and therefore replace all the others. Consequently, he installed expensive machinery and equipment in his factory. This included a perfectly smooth glass table on which the film was prepared and cut into strips. The costly investment was worthwhile because just two years after its invention, film was spooled and sold as rolls. This meant that photographers did not have to return the camera to be reloaded with film – they just bought a new roll from a Kodak supplier.

It was not long before the factory was struggling to keep up with the demand for the new film.

Kodak advertising encouraged people to think of idyllic situations where a camera would keep a permanent record of good times. It still adopts a similar tactic today with beaches and family gatherings being snapped on Kodak film.

Big, bigger, biggest

During the time that the Kodak camera was really becoming established in the United States, George Eastman was exploring commercial possibilities in various other parts of the world. He saw the whole world as one enormous market place.

The Eastman Photographic Materials Company Limited was established in London, England, in 1889. It was through this outlet that products that had been manufactured in the United States were distributed to Europe, the Far East, and Australia.

Above and right: Hand-tinted photographs of the late nineteenth century. Touch-up artists were hired to enliven black and white photographs. Images like these were in great demand as people became increasingly curious about far-off lands, such as China and Russia, and their peoples. Eastman was able to tap into this market and photography continues to bring different cultures alive today.

Two years later, the worldwide demand for cameras and films was so great that a manufacturing factory was built on the outskirts of London. During the 1890s Kodak set up in Paris as Kodak SAF and in Berlin as Kodak GMBH.

The London factory was built at around the same time as a major upheaval in Rochester. Tired of forever moving to larger premises as the business expanded, Eastman purchased a plot of land not far from the city and built a factory complex that became known as Kodak Park.

In 1892, realizing that his pet word, Kodak, was at least as significant as his own name, he changed the company to the Eastman Kodak Company.

All over the world

During the 1880s, all Eastman products had been sold in "sole agency" outlets. These were quite often pharmacies owned and run by a single person – and were specially selected to stock and sell Eastman Kodak products. Each outlet was guaranteed a distribution area where there would be no rivals. This also meant that Eastman Kodak was saved the expense of having to purchase properties and pay staff to run them.

By the early 1890s, however, when Eastman was in his late thirties, he had a change of heart and considered that it would be worthwhile for Kodak to have its own distribution outlets. These outlets would be owned by Kodak, but run and operated as separate companies. All the companies would bear the name of Kodak – and therefore publicize the name even more – and would sell Kodak products, both to the general public as well as to other businesses and professionals.

It was not long before Kodak businesses could be found all over the world – by the turn of the century there were Kodak outlets in France, Germany, Australia, and Egypt. All were immaculate.

Eastman was anxious to convey quality; the last thing he wanted was for his products to be tarnished by the appearance of an untidy showroom. In many of the establishments, customers were encouraged to

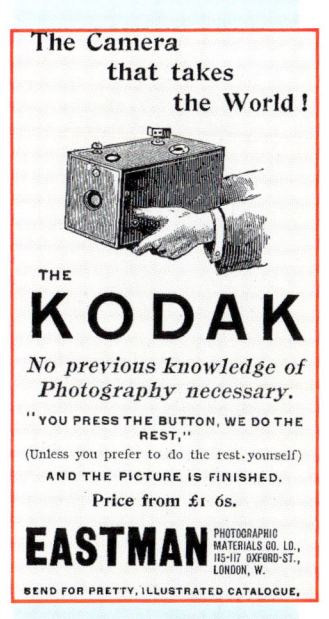

Above: An 1893 British advertisement for the Kodak camera, emphasizing its simplicity.

Below: A box of Newman's Photographic paints that were used to tint daguerreotypes and other early photographic prints.

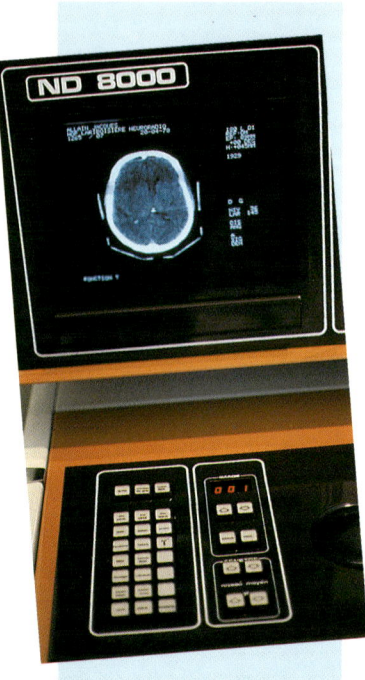

watch a free demonstration in the ways of photography – just a quick show to convince them that it was a simple and enjoyable pastime. It all worked like a dream and people were easily swayed and more than willing to purchase a camera on their way out.

Keeping pace

George Eastman wanted the word Kodak to be familiar to absolutely everyone – from children to royalty. But he did not want the product to be cheapened in any way – far from it – he wanted Kodak to be associated with everything that was perceived to be good in the world.

By the middle of the 1890s, over one hundred thousand Kodak cameras had been sold and three hundred miles of film were being manufactured every month. Eastman's dogged determination to achieve his goal of making photography universally popular had succeeded at last.

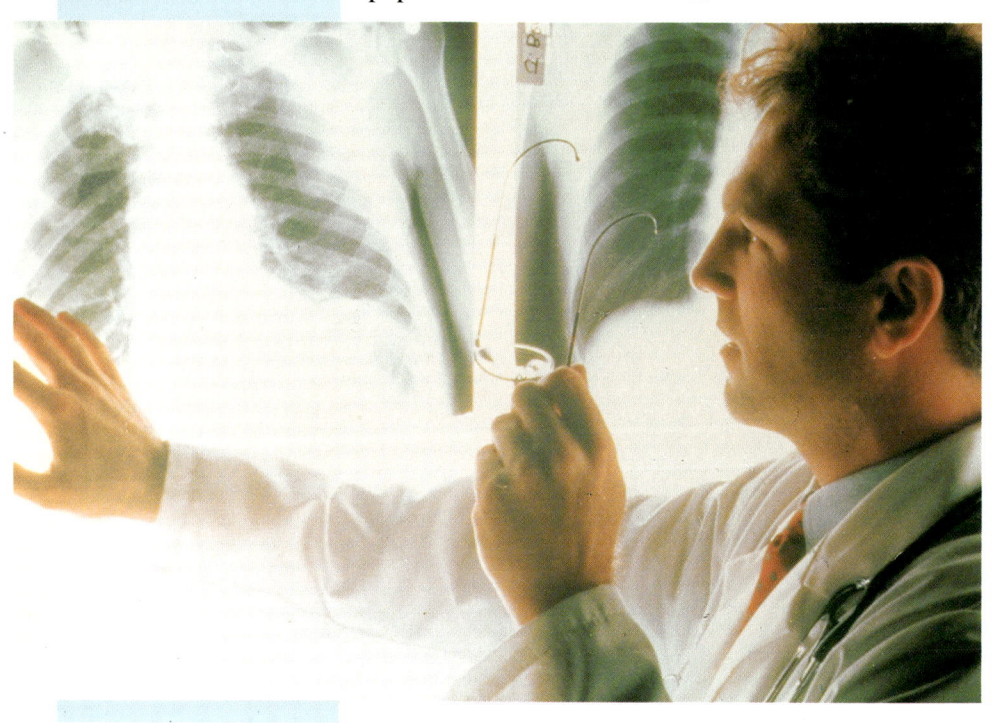

Most of the photographs taken were of relatives or family gatherings, but photography was also being used in many diverse and less obvious ways.

In 1895, a German physicist named Wilhelm Roentgen discovered X-rays. The benefits of X-rays were quickly established and as soon as it was realized that they could be developed as photographs, Eastman became interested. A year later, in 1896, Kodak was producing commercially available X-ray plates.

During the 1890s, the inventor of the gramophone, Thomas Edison, had been toying with the idea of making a movie camera. One of the problems that confronted Edison – and others like him who were interested in making movie cameras – was that most film was inadequate in one way or another. The film had to be strong and transparent and it was not until Edison discovered Eastman's new film that he found what he was looking for.

Edison produced a "Kinetoscope," which was the forerunner of the modern movie camera. This invention, coupled with the new Eastman film, marked the arrival of the film industry. This new industry would not only have a huge impact on ordinary people's lives, but would also create a colossal new market for Eastman's products.

As Thomas Edison and like-minded inventors continued to improve the development of the movie camera, Eastman made sure that Kodak kept up with the pace by continually marketing improved films. The demand for movie, or "cine" film as it was known, was so great that Kodak found it difficult to produce enough.

Above: A candid snap of the man who made photography available to millions. Eastman, thirty-six years old, was going to Europe by ship when a fellow passenger caught him lining up a photograph with his own Kodak box camera.

Opposite top: For years Kodak was involved in researching medical technology. Here, a sophisticated scanner projects the image of a skull onto a screen.

Opposite bottom: A year after X-rays were discovered in 1895, Kodak broke into the new market with the first X-ray plates.

New designs

Although George Eastman was the driving force behind Kodak, a man named Frank Brownell also played an important role. He was a camera designer who made cameras for Kodak while also running his own company. Eastman, always a thoughtful employer and kind friend, praised Brownell, saying that he was "The greatest camera designer the world has known."

Main picture: A Kodak industrial complex in the United States. During the 1990s Kodak made concerted efforts to save energy and minimize pollution.

During his seventeen-year association with Kodak, Brownell made and designed some sixty different types of camera. Among the most important of these were the Folding Kodak and the Pocket Kodak. Until these came on to the market, the vast majority of cameras were box-shaped and consequently fairly cumbersome. Not only did these new cameras fold in half, collapsing like bellows, but their films were contained in cartridges and could therefore be loaded and unloaded in daylight.

The Folding Pocket Kodak was another best-selling design of Brownell's and was genuinely small enough to be folded up and slipped into a pocket. Just five years later nearly one and a half million Kodak cameras had been sold and film was being

Inset top and bottom: A city within a city. Aerial photographs of modern Kodak factories in England.

produced at the rate of four hundred miles per month. This increasing growth in sales enabled Kodak to continue its policy of expansion.

Kodak took over other companies, buying them outright for lump sums. More often than not, these companies were moved – equipment, personnel, everything – to Kodak Park.

Kodak also bought patents so that it had the ownership rights to other products or inventions. To a slightly nervous Henry Strong, it seemed that the company was growing too fast and he feared that sales would start to decline and that the company would collapse.

Strong trusted Eastman, however, and was reassured when Eastman told him that the only way forward for Kodak was to reinvest money in the company.

A camera for a dollar

It had always been part of Eastman's strategy to promote new products, foster good ideas, and buy machinery to make his factories more efficient. While many feared that Kodak would be weakened by its speedy growth, believing that there just was not the market for all its products, Eastman was convinced that he had only touched the tip of the iceberg. He was sure that the best way to succeed was to continually improve and increase the range of products and to keep one step ahead of any company attempting to compete. He advised Strong, "If we can get out improved goods every year nobody will be able to follow us and compete with us."

Some people felt that, as Kodak became bigger and there was no real opposition in the world of photography, the huge company was monopolizing the business. This meant that Kodak could dictate the price of photography. People thought that Kodak would increase its prices.

Eastman, however, was striving to do the exact opposite – he wanted to make photography as cheap as possible and his specific desire was to manufacture a camera that could be sold for just $1.

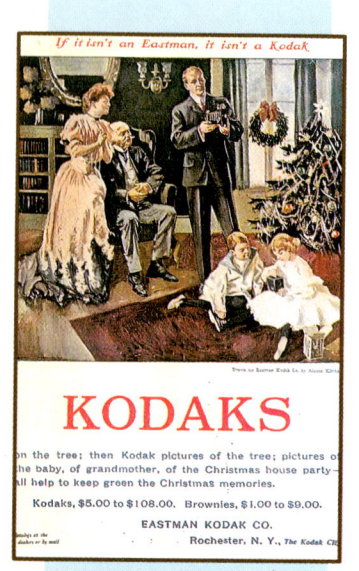

Cameras for all ages: father ponders his expensive folding camera while his children unwrap their new Brownie. After the advent of the Brownie in 1900, Christmas time proved to be an annual bonanza for Kodak as children craved to be given one as a gift. The slogan, "If it isn't an Eastman, it isn't a Kodak," reinforced loyalty to the Eastman cameras.

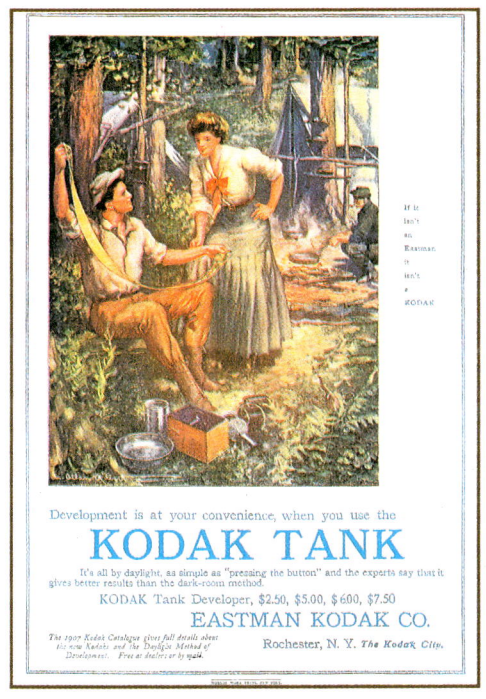

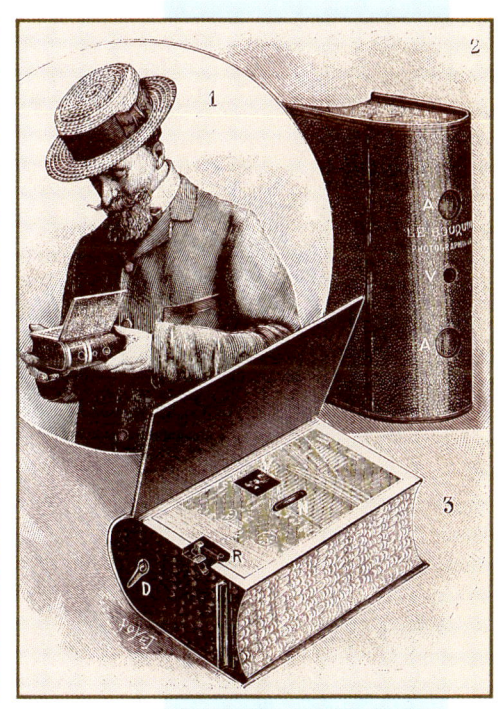

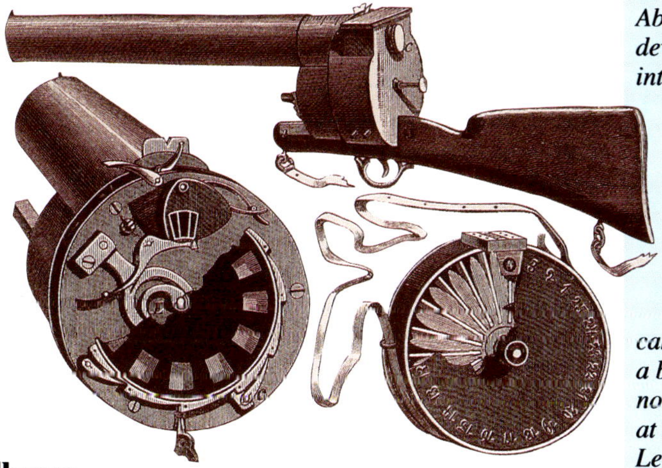

Above, left: The Kodak developing tank, introduced in 1902, made it possible for enthusiasts to develop roll film outside a conventional darkroom.
Above right: An ingenious spy camera in the shape of a book. Many such novelties were produced at the turn of the century.
Left: In 1882, the French scientist, E.J. Marey, designed a clockwork-driven camera in the shape of a gun to photograph movement.

Shares

The year 1898 saw the union of the British company of Eastman Photographic Materials and the Eastman Kodak Company of New York when it became one single company named simply Kodak Limited.

Kodak Limited owned everything that was Kodak, all over the world – patents, copyrights, outlets, factories, and equipment. It was decided that the new company should be located in London, England, the commercial capital of the world at the time, and that it should become a public company. This meant that people would be able to invest in it by buying shares. The money from the shares would be used to make the business more profitable.

It came as no surprise when shares in Kodak Limited were sold out as soon as they were put on the market. With the huge influx of money from the shareholders, Kodak Limited had enormous resources at its disposal and George Eastman once again looked to the future.

The first "divvy"

As the company got bigger and bigger, Eastman was obliged to spend less time experimenting with ideas and more time making business decisions. However, he frequently walked around the factories, chatting to his employees as he went. He made it obvious to all his workers that they could approach him if they stumbled across a problem.

Pioneering good relations with his staff, he went one step further and actively encouraged his work force to come up with ideas that might improve efficiency. As an incentive, he offered bonuses for smart suggestions.

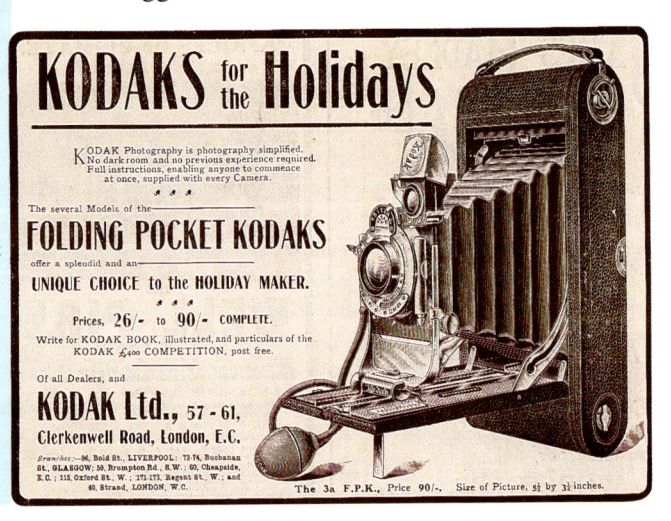

Above: Kodak first produced an annual list of its products in 1895. What might have simply been a boring list of goods turned into a lavishly illustrated publication and by 1910 it became famous as The Catalog and sold more than a million copies a year. This cover of the 1915 Catalog epitomizes the style and elegance that were the fashion at the time.

Right: Kodak targeted specific markets for each new range of cameras it produced. This 1905 British advertisement for Kodak's ingenious folding cameras was aimed at the humble tourist.

A year after introducing the suggestions system, Eastman made another decision that was considered equally astounding – he shared with his employees the huge personal profit that he had made when the company was put on the stock market. At the time, this was a novel move, but Eastman believed that his employees contributed to the success of Kodak and therefore deserved some kind of reward. He had founded the company on mutual respect between employees and employer.

In all, Eastman dispensed $178,000 among around three thousand people in what he called the "divvy." As the company grew, the divvy was formalized into a profit-sharing scheme. George Eastman thought it only fair that if the company made a profit at the end of a year's trading, then the workers, as well as the shareholders, should benefit.

Thank you, Mr. Brownell

Soon after the dawn of the twentieth century, the wizard camera designer Frank Brownell came up with a design that satisfied all Eastman's requirements.

It was named the Brownie after Brownell and within a year nearly a quarter of a million had been sold. The Brownie was extremely basic but this was exactly why it was a success. The design was so good that it remained much the same for

Above: At the turn of the century, the public was still wary of photography so Kodak outlets offered free demonstrations to coax people to come into the stores and to spend money.
Below: The most famous camera of them all – the Brownie.

approximately eighty years. Unlike any other camera, the Brownie was made specifically for children and its sales potential was ruthlessly exploited: Brownie clubs were organized, photographic competitions were arranged and the "Brownie Boy" featured in numerous magazine and newspaper advertisements.

Perhaps the most important thing about the Brownie, besides its simple and effective design, was its price. It cost just $1. A film cartridge containing six exposures cost fifteen cents and it cost a mere forty-five cents to get prints made up. Eastman had achieved his $1 ambition.

Above: Kodak employees were hard-working and loyal and they had every reason to be. George Eastman encouraged a positive attitude and productive work place.

Below: A French illustration of early film-makers shooting footage of a battle.

Looking after the work force

In 1904 George Eastman reduced his employees' working hours – from ten to nine hours a day – with no loss of pay. He believed that this was no more than his efficient employees deserved.

More good news for the Kodak work force was to follow. It had been known for some time that the chemical used by Kodak as a base for film, cellulose nitrate, was flammable. This had been discovered when a stock of X-ray films had caught fire. With a concern for safety, Kodak started to produce films that were not potentially lethal and it successfully manufactured a safety film in 1908. This concern for safety had further effects as well.

In 1911, Eastman created an accident, benefit, and pension fund for all his employees, who now numbered over five thousand. Furthermore, a Kodak committee was formed to look into accident prevention. This was a wise precaution as many of the chemicals and compounds used in the production of films were extremely poisonous.

A private man

George Eastman never married; he devoted almost all of his life to his business. It has been said that he had little time for recreation before he was fifty years old. His life and character were full of contradictions – he was a tough, competitive businessman yet capable of extraordinary acts of generosity. He made photography universally popular, yet was so unassuming and modest that few photographs were ever taken of him.

To relax, George Eastman liked nothing more than to tinker in his workshop or to carry out repairs at his hunting lodge in North Carolina. He loved to fish, read, and listen to music. He was not the sort of person to loll around in the sun when he wasn't working. He preferred to remain active and went on safari in Africa and camping expeditions with friends.

Music was a lifelong passion of Eastman's, although he had no musical ability himself. He had an organ in his home and he liked having someone play to him

George Eastman worked hard and played hard. To relax, he liked nothing more than to go camping with close friends. He particularly enjoyed his status as a superb camp cook

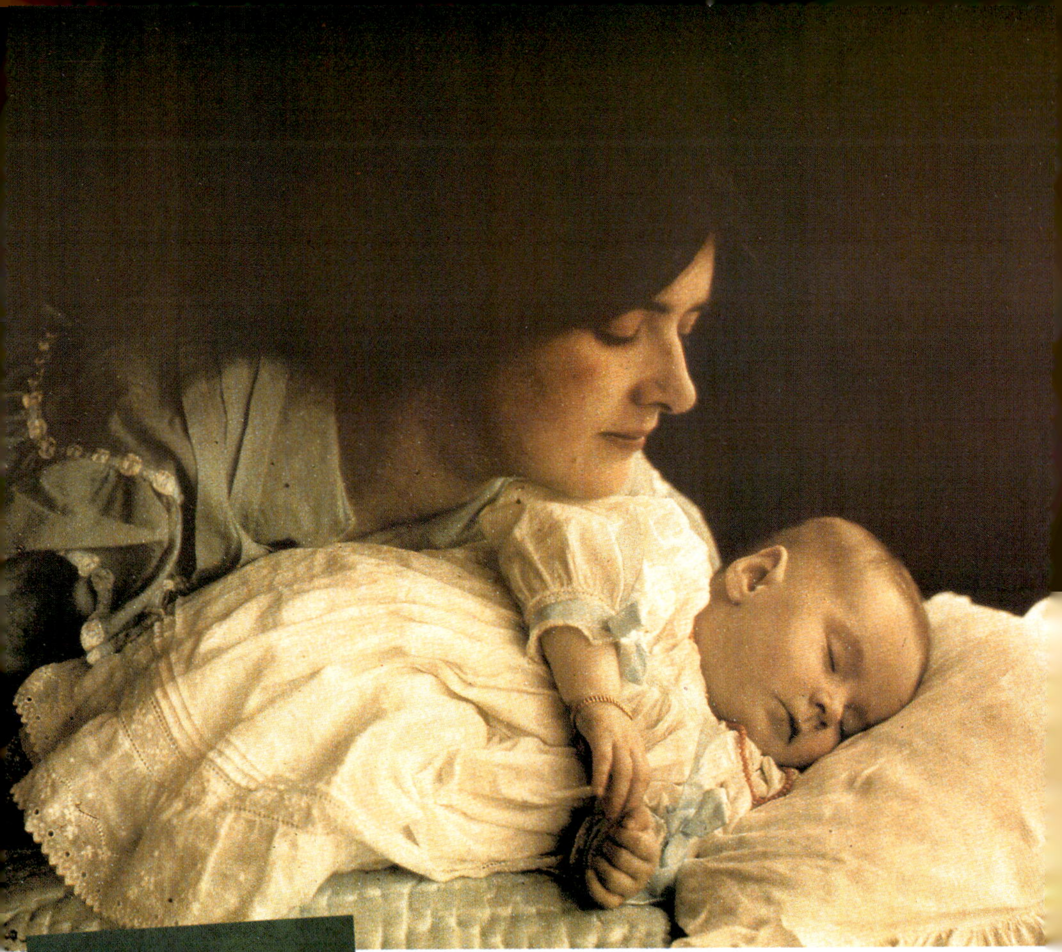

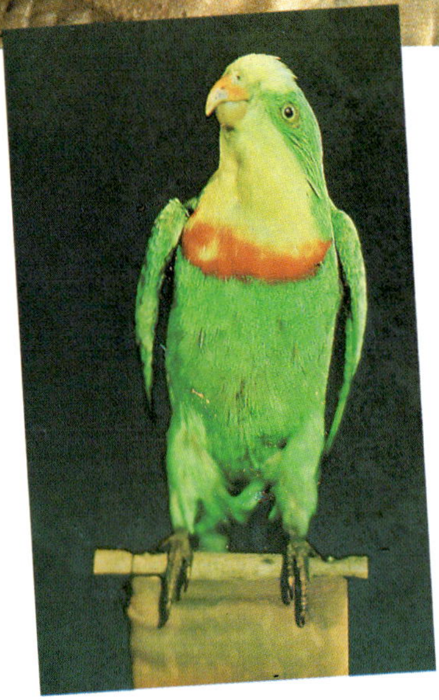

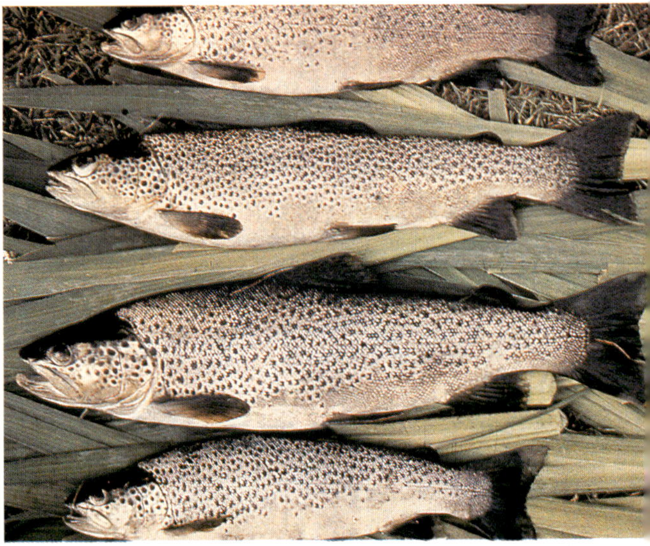

while he ate his meals. He founded and sponsored the Rochester Symphony Orchestra as well as the University of Rochester's Eastman School of Music.

Another interest was medicine. Eastman helped establish a school of medicine and a hospital at the University of Rochester and he also founded a dental clinic. This dental clinic was so popular that similar clinics were set up all over Europe – in London, Paris, Rome, Stockholm, and Brussels. In 1994, the London clinic was still England's foremost dental research and education unit.

You can always get what you want

By the end of 1911, George Eastman was shown around the chemicals factory of a German company, Bayer. It was revealed that the German company employed several hundred research scientists. Eastman was loathe to admit that Kodak employed a mere ten chemists.

Eastman determined to change the situation, realizing that Kodak was only going to fall behind other companies in developing products if it did not have the right staff to carry out necessary research. A scientist who would be capable of establishing a Kodak research laboratory was needed.

Eventually the name of an Englishman was put forward – Dr. Charles Mees, who, although only thirty years old, was joint managing director of a small but successful photographic firm named Wratten and Wainwright.

Eastman approached Charles Mees with the offer of a job and he accepted without hesitation. However, remembering his partners at Wratten and Wainwright, he knew that the company would probably stop production if he left. Mees told Eastman that if he wanted him, he would have to buy Wratten and Wainwright as well. In an extraordinarily flamboyant gesture, Eastman agreed and bought the entire English company.

All the employees of Wratten and Wainwright were offered similar jobs at Kodak Limited, in England. There was no loss of jobs and everybody was happy – most of all, George Eastman.

Opposite: Scientists and photographers alike were keen to produce images showing the different tones and hues of real life. As early as 1861, scientists were able to prove that this was possible. The process was complex, so for many years black and white photographs were hand-tinted. The four trout (opposite, bottom right) used platinum processing – to highlight different tones in a black and white print. Gradually, a process involving red and green was invented (opposite, bottom left). By 1907, a system using autochrome plates was developed. This used red, green and blue (opposite top). The results of such processes, however, were difficult to guarantee, giving rise to many faults in the pictures themselves.

"What we do in our working hours determines what we have; what we do in our leisure hours determines what we are."

George Eastman.

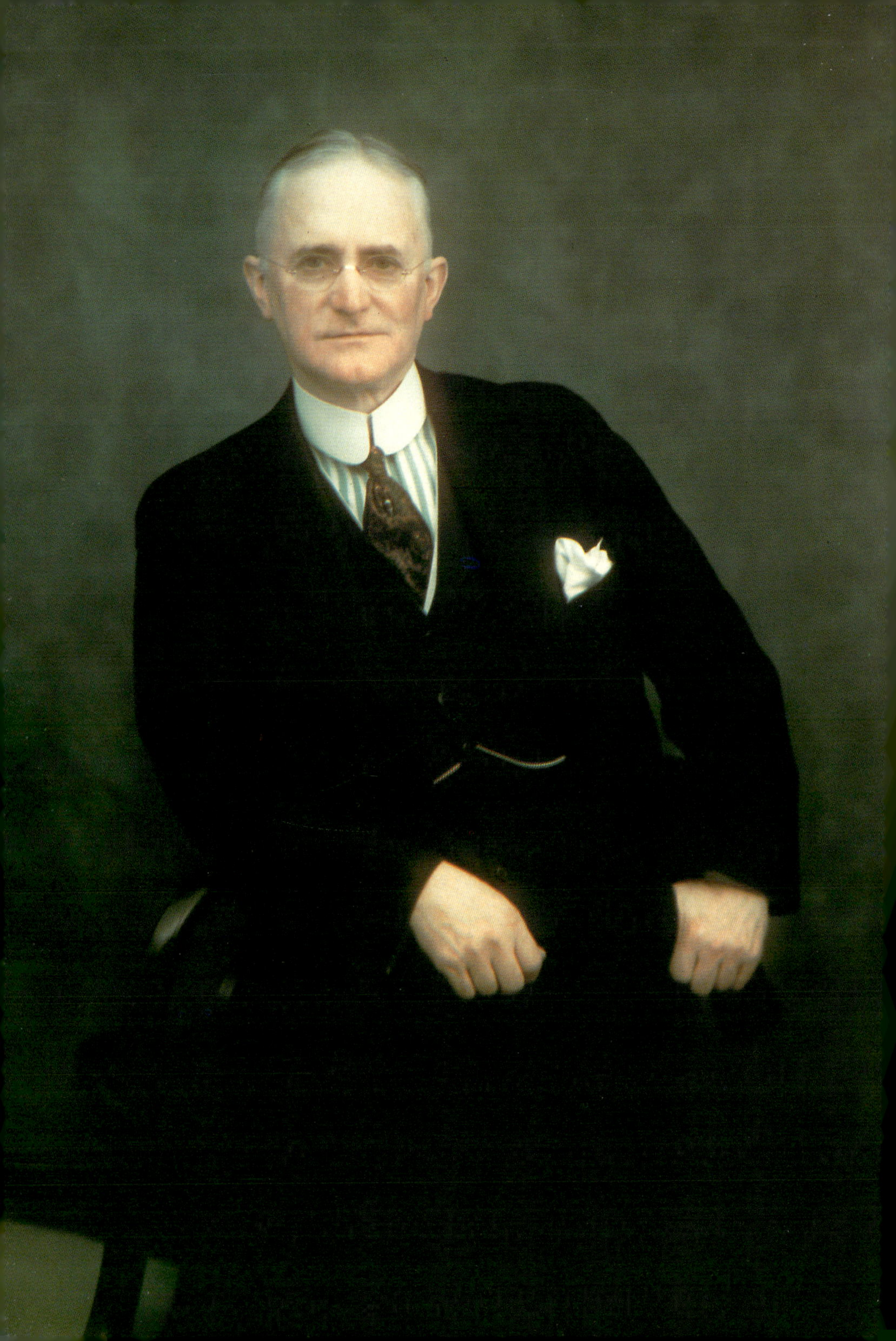

The following year, in another flamboyant gesture, Eastman gave one and a half million dollars worth of Kodak stock to a university that he had always admired and which had supplied a number of skilled Kodak employees, the Massachusetts Institute of Technology (M.I.T.) The donation was made in the name of "Smith," and people wondered who the mysterious Mr. Smith really was. "What I desire to avoid as far as possible is the notoriety which oftentimes accompanies such gifts," he explained. It was only after eight years of annoying speculation that Eastman let it be known that he was the generous donor. By the time of his death, Eastman was reputed to have given more than $20 million to M.I.T.

> "So far as we know, Mr. Eastman was the first manufacturer in the United States to formulate and put into practice the modern policy of large-scale production at low costs for a world market, backed by scientific research and extensive advertising."
>
> Dr. E. Seligman, from C. W. Ackerman's biography, George Eastman.

Mees gets to work

During 1912, Mees moved to America and started to organize the construction of a research facility at Kodak Park. He brought several tried and trusted colleagues from England with him – the "English Invasion," as the locals in Rochester called it.

At the beginning of 1913, the building was ready and the scientists went to work. This was one of the first commercial research laboratories to be established in the United States.

Eastman encouraged Mees to research whatever he liked. Eastman outlined his job description: "Your mission is the future of photography." To some this might have been intimidating, but Mees considered it to be the chance he had been waiting for, for years. However, he did warn Eastman not to expect too much too soon, saying that it would probably be about ten years before he and his team came up with anything that would be of any use.

Mees was not entirely right. They soon produced a high-contrast X-ray film that had commercial potential. Also, by the year 1914 a new film named Kodachrome was developed by a fellow scientist John Capstaff. The development of Kodachrome was exciting as it used red and green rather than just black and white. However, the printed results were satisfactory for portraits, but were of limited use for other subjects.

Opposite: A portrait of George Eastman taken in 1914, when he was sixty years old. He was still working hard at the Eastman Kodak company and was encouraging research in the new area of movies. Eastman did not stop working until he was seventy-one.

Hannibal makes a comeback

Trouble loomed for Kodak in 1913 – the patent that had been disputed in 1889 by the Reverend Hannibal Goodwin reared its ugly head again. Goodwin had died in 1900 and his firm, the Goodwin Film and Camera Company, had been taken over by a large concern, Ansco. Eastman had tried to resolve the problem of who owned the patent, but it was not a simple matter – over the years various judges had been baffled by lawyers arguing about complicated chemical formulae. The matter was finally resolved when Kodak was ordered to pay Ansco $5 million.

Eastman was angered by the decision but was glad to be free of the problem. In exchange for the huge sum of money, Kodak was granted the right to use Goodwin's patented product.

But more legal disputes were to follow. The U.S. Attorney General warned Kodak that it was looking into the possibility that Kodak was becoming a monopoly and had been buying up other companies

A hand-tinted photograph used to promote Kodak film and printing-out paper. The happy family was a theme that Eastman liked. This was not because he was a family man himself – he never married – but because it was a good sales technique aimed at a growing market.

so that it could dictate product prices and wipe out competing companies.

George Eastman refuted the allegations, but the Attorney General's office filed suit against Kodak. Two years later it was decided that the Eastman Kodak company was in fact a monopoly. Kodak immediately appealed the decision and another saga of legal wrangling began.

The war years

When World War I had started in 1914, Kodak's businesses in Europe came to a virtual standstill, but trade within the United States was hardly affected.

However, when the United States declared war on Germany in 1917, the deeply patriotic George Eastman offered his services, and those of his company, to the government. The War Department was quick to accept Kodak's offer to supply the chemical that was used to make film base to waterproof the fragile wings of aircraft. However, it was slow to pick up Eastman's idea of developing aerial photography.

It was not long, though, before commanders recognized that photographs could play an important role in documenting and planning strategies on the ground. In the spring of 1918, a school of aerial photography opened in Rochester and by the end of the war, in the November of that year, more than a million aerial photographs had been taken from planes flying over the battlefields of northern France.

Just as the United States entered the war, Kodak brought out a camera that was advertised as "The Soldier's Kodak Camera" – it was specifically made for the young men who were destined to cross the Atlantic to fight.

Boom years

In a strange way, photography was promoted by World War I. By the time peace was declared in 1919, people all over the world were familiar with snapshots. Although comparatively few pictures were taken of actual fighting, many thousands were

Above: Life in the trenches before the Battle of Ypres, 1917. Pictures taken during World War I did much to promote photography and Kodak was not alone in enjoying a boom period after peace had been declared in 1918.

Kodak and the Technicolor Corporation joined forces to make dramatic strides in the quality of moviemaking. The fanciful sets and costumes in The Wizard of Oz *(1939) exploited the latest in technology to the full and mesmerized the moviegoing public.*

taken of loved ones at home and of friends setting off to the front. Photographs of political leaders and generals were regularly published in daily newspapers and so photography became an accepted part of daily life.

In 1920, Kodak sold five times as many cameras as it had in 1914, when the war started. To boost this new enthusiasm for photography, Kodak initiated massive advertising campaigns.

As business boomed Eastman Kodak soon made a significant move – it created a company named the Tennessee Eastman Company. The company manufactured the wood alcohol from which film base was made – this made perfect business sense from Kodak's point of view since it meant that it no longer needed to buy wood alcohol from another company.

Within ten years the Tennessee Eastman Company would be making a whole range of Kodak products that had little or nothing to do with photography.

The post-war years were also a golden age for the movies. Moviemaking had come a long way in twenty years. In 1903, the silent movie classic *The Great Train Robbery* was made. It lasted just fifteen minutes, but this was considered such a long time that notices were posted outside where the film was being shown to warn potential customers that they might get bored!

Twenty years later, however, movies lasting an hour or more could hardly be produced fast enough to satisfy the demand from the American and European public. Since Kodak supplied most of the Hollywood moviemakers with film, the industry proved to be a huge source of revenue for the company.

Early in the 1920s, Kodak forged a working relationship with the Technicolor Corporation. Between them, the two companies made significant advances over the years in the lucrative world of moviemaking and they took out patents on each new development they made. This eventually led to a clash with the United States government, which accused the two businesses of conspiring to take absolute control of cinematography. Confrontation with the government or not, many years later Kodak received the ultimate accolade when it was awarded an Oscar for its contribution to the movie industry.

But while Hollywood was establishing itself as the place for professional moviemaking, Eastman sensed there might be a similar market for amateur moviemaking closer to home.

The movie industry enjoyed a golden age after World War I and the number of movies being made soared. Kodak consequently reaped rich rewards as the company produced the bulk of the film used in Hollywood.

Home movies

After many years of research and experimentation in 1923, Kodak released a practical home movies camera – the Cine-Kodak Motion Picture Camera together with the Kodascope projector. The problem with the new camera was its high price compared with a still camera.

Not surprisingly, sales were slow at first, but many people started to use the camera for photographing things other than family get-togethers. Operations were filmed in hospitals so that new techniques could be passed on to students. And, for the first time, films were used in schools – this led to the creation of a new Kodak company, the Eastman Teaching Films Corporation.

The Cine-Kodak system was still black and white, however, and George Eastman desperately wanted to change that. Spurred on by Eastman himself, Kodak researchers came up with Kodacolor film in 1928. This new technology was launched in an ingenious way by Eastman. He held a party at his Rochester home and invited the country's most important leaders and industrialists, including his old friend Thomas Edison, to attend.

During the afternoon of the party, each guest was given the opportunity to use a camera loaded with Kodacolor. In an interlude, the films were developed and were then shown to the gathering in the evening. To Eastman's delight, Kodacolor received universal approval and, as was his way, many complimentary remarks were noted and used as testimonials to promote the film when it went on sale. One problem with Kodacolor was, however, that it could not be reprinted – only one edition could be made – so its use was limited to home movies.

A good place to work

One of the most remarkable things about George Eastman was that he never forgot his work force or took it for granted. He was a tough businessman and hard negotiator, but he always appreciated hard work and he went further than the vast majority of employers to help his employees.

He had given a third of his Kodak shares to his fifteen thousand employees in 1919 and he had introduced the Eastman Savings and Loan Association, which encouraged employees to save money. He had also made it possible for men and women to take out loans so that they could buy their own homes.

An exclusive insurance scheme was also initiated. An employee could take out a policy that would guarantee a pension at retirement or a lump sum payment in the event of death or a disabling accident.

Top: Eastman and Edison (right).

Bottom: Touring with a Kodak.

Few other companies paid out an annual divvy if they had a successful year and fewer still offered savings and insurance plans. In return for these benefits, Eastman expected – and got – loyalty and commitment from his work force.

George Eastman relaxing at home in his library. Despite amassing a fortune and making photography universally popular, he remained a private man throughout his life.

New roles

In 1923, when George Eastman was sixty-nine years old, he handed over the running of the Eastman Kodak company and became chairman of the board of directors. It was his duty to hear his fellow directors' ideas and to put decisions into practice.

Eager to remain active he headed off on a safari, in 1926, to collect specimens for the American Museum of Natural History. He enjoyed the safari so much that he repeated his trip the following year when he was seventy-three. He fully intended to give Eastman Kodak and its management room to develop without his domineering presence.

Eastman kept himself fully occupied with his numerous personal interests but, with age, became increasingly inactive. He began to suffer from

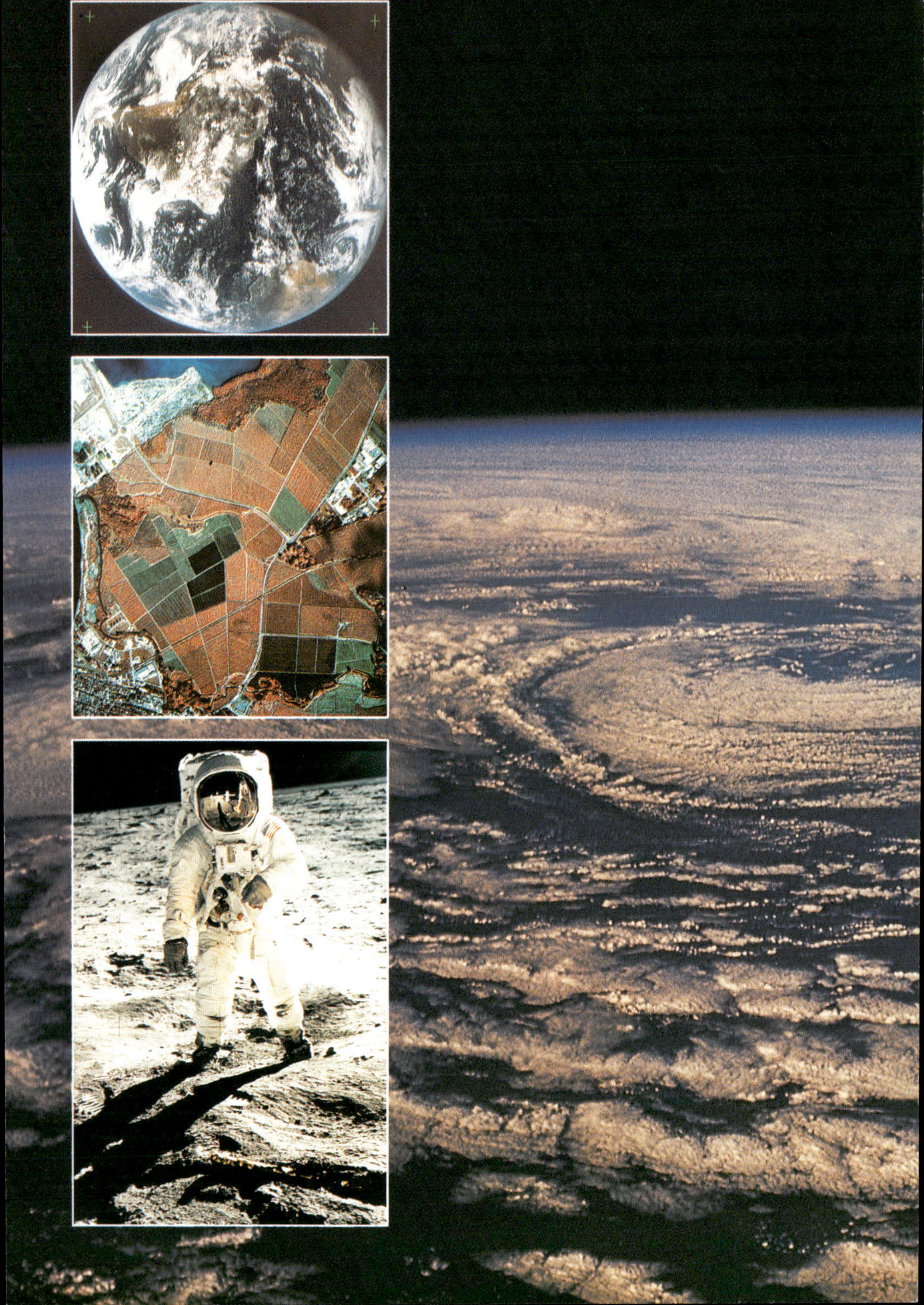

arteriosclerosis, hardening of the arteries. He found movement difficult and became increasingly frustrated as he slowly had to give up his active lifestyle. He dreaded a long-lasting illness in which he would lose his mental and physical abilities.

Meanwhile, Eastman gave his approval for some novel publicity ideas, such as the Kodak Hour. This radio show extolled the wonders of photography in general and Kodak in particular. It was aimed at the whole family and became such a huge success that further shows, the Kodak Weekend Hour and the Kodak Mid-Week Hour followed.

During the years that they were broadcast, Kodak produced a range of inexpensive cameras to suit different age groups – there were cameras for teenagers, fashionable ones for fashionable adults, and even a plastic one called the Baby Brownie.

Main picture: The extraordinary view of a hurricane taken from an orbiting satellite using Kodak photographic equipment and film.
Opposite top: An image of the Earth at a height of 22,300 miles.
Opposite middle: A high-altitude photograph of farmland next to industrial towns.
Opposite bottom: Buzz Aldrin snapped on Kodak film by Neil Armstrong, the first men to land on the moon.

The Massachussetts Institute in Technology. Eastman was extremely generous to organizations that he felt could benefit the whole of society. M.I.T. provided Kodak with quite a number of employees. Eastman felt an investment in the future development of industry was good not only for Kodak, but for the United States as a whole.

Compassion

For many years, George Eastman had been an immensely wealthy man, but he saw little point in hoarding money away. He preferred to put it to good use and during the latter half of his life he gave away the bulk of his fortune. He could also see that it would be easier for the company if he had disposed of his wealth and shares before his death.

Eastman wanted better opportunities to be available for the black people of America. He accordingly sponsored the Hampton and Tuskegee Institutes, which educated black people in teaching and community work. On occasion, Eastman's generosity started adverse speculation and publicity. After a particularly generous spree in 1923, it had been believed that he was about to retire and he was forced to issue a reassuring statement to his staff that also gave an account of his donations:

M.I.T.	$4,500,000
University of Rochester	
School of Music	$3,000,000
College of Arts and Science	$2,500,000
Medical School	$1,500,000
College for Women	$1,500,000
Hampton Institute	$1,000,000
Tuskegee Institute	$1,000,000

By the 1930s, Eastman had long since retired from the Kodak empire. He was still acutely interested in what was happening, but he left routine managerial decisions to others. His illness had progressed and, on March 14, 1932, he invited some friends around to witness an amendment to his will that gave most of his remaining wealth to the University of Rochester. After signing the document, Eastman went upstairs and shot himself. He left a note saying, "My work is done. Why wait?" He ended his life in the controlled, orderly way in which he had lived it.

Perhaps the most impressive thing about George Eastman was that he managed to be both a successful inventor and a successful businessman – a very rare combination. There is barely a place on earth where his famous company is not known.

Progress

Eastman died at a time of change within the photographic world. The days of the hit and miss experiments to discover new emulsions and formulae were long gone. New cameras and films were now the products of intense scientific research. But, as Mees had predicted, the research laboratory did not come up with best-selling products immediately.

The scope of research that took place at Rochester and other Kodak laboratories became increasingly diverse. Cameras, film bases, emulsions, lenses, and chemicals were all studied and this led to a snowball effect – as more research was carried out, more viable products were discovered and ultimately manufactured, if not by Eastman Kodak, then by one of its increasing number of subsidiary companies.

"If a man has wealth, he has to make a choice.... He can keep it together in a bunch and then leave it for others to administer after he is dead, or, he can get it into action and have fun, while he is still alive. I prefer getting it into action and adapting it to human needs, and making the plan work."

George Eastman, from Hearst International magazine, 1923.

"George Eastman is among the comparatively few men of the last generation who can unreservedly be called great for outstanding, constructive and lasting achievements."

From George Eastman, a Kodak publication.

53

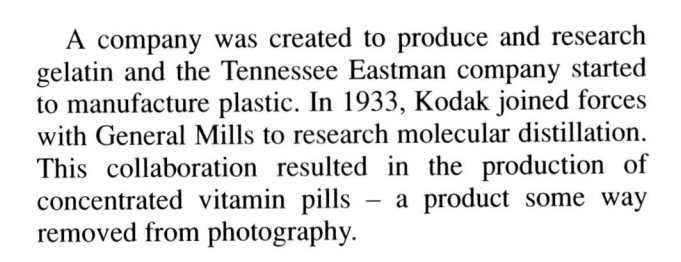

A company was created to produce and research gelatin and the Tennessee Eastman company started to manufacture plastic. In 1933, Kodak joined forces with General Mills to research molecular distillation. This collaboration resulted in the production of concentrated vitamin pills – a product some way removed from photography.

Breakthrough at last!

The breakthrough that Mees and his team had been so anxious to achieve for so long, finally came in 1935. Two slightly eccentric, but brilliant scientists succeeded in producing a film that used red, green, and blue named Kodachrome after its predecessor.

This product was far superior to anything that had gone before. To start with, Kodak processed all the Kodachrome film to a new size and returned it in strips to the photographer. However, in 1938, the strips were cut and were returned in cardboard windows which went under the trademark of Readymount. At the same time, the Kodaslide projector was manufactured and between them, these two products made the new sized film, 35mm, universally popular.

In 1939, a photography world fair was held in New York and Kodak proudly showed its Hall of Color. In the middle was a giant screen onto which transparencies were projected. The visiting public had never seen anything like it and both amateurs and professionals were stunned by the display. The resulting publicity was impressive, but unfortunately Kodak euphoria was short-lived. World War II had begun.

Kodak was fully prepared and ready to help the war effort. This time, unlike during World War I, the government was pleased to receive all offers of assistance.

Eastman Kodak had impressive research scientists and facilities. The chemical company, Tennessee Eastman, produced synthetic yarns to replace silk and wool. It also manufactured huge quantities of the devastating explosive RDX, which was used in bombs and torpedoes. Kodak also made bomb fuses and some of its research scientists worked on the atomic bomb project.

So much of Kodak's output was directed to the war effort that production of commercial products slowed to a virtual standstill. In 1943, no cameras were produced for amateur use at all.

When the fighting came to a halt in 1945, the public, which had been deprived of taking photographs for so long, became "snap happy." Kodak was not slow to take up the challenge to supply the market with new products and new ideas.

In the five years following the war Kodak invested heavily in updating equipment. In 1949 a new Kodacolor film was launched onto the market but was surprisingly slow to take off.

What it's like to be famous! The cameras are probably Japanese or German, but the films inside them are most likely to be made by Kodak. Photography, since Eastman started working on the individual processes in his mother's kitchen over one hundred years ago, has changed into quite a different media product and all due to the drive and vision of one man.

Opposite: Kodak film – just part of Eastman's legacy to photography.

55

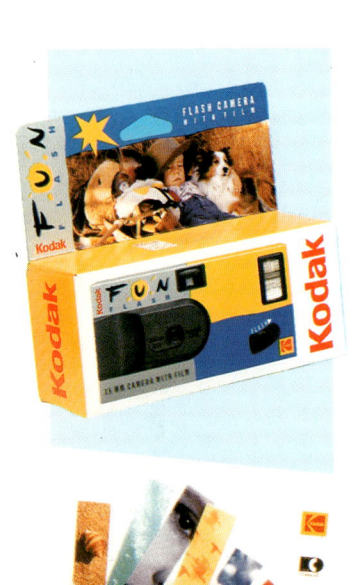

Determined to make the film sell better, Kodak started an advertising blitz and took every opportunity it could to promote its products.

In 1950 the company was approached to decorate the vast hallway of New York's Grand Central Station. The result was the first of many "Colorama" transparencies that were back-projected onto a huge screen. The Colorama was viewed by 650,000 people every day, but what was more important was that magazines and newspapers often featured items on the Colorama. Every time this happened, Kodak received free publicity. The Colorama was only removed in 1989 when Grand Central Station was renovated.

In 1951, Kodak set up more research facilities in the United States, as well as new ones in England, France, and Australia.

Instamatics

In the mid-1960s Kodak employed over 100,000 people all over the world and worldwide sales topped $2 billion for the first time. However, Japanese and German 35mm cameras were making deep inroads into the traditional Kodak market. So Kodak developed its Instamatic range of cameras. George Eastman would have approved of the Instamatic. It echoed the essential designs of the first Brownie.

It came in various grades of sophistication – the most expensive had built-in flash units, and light meters. All were compact, simple to use and, above all, reliable. Film came in a plastic cartridge and was foolproof to load and unload. Even the camera's name suited the heady days of the sixties. More than seventy million Instamatics were sold. The Pocket Instamatic resulted in a further twenty-five million sales.

In 1976, Kodak went into what appeared to be the lucrative market of instant photography. It manufactured cameras and a special film that developed snapshots into prints soon after exposure. Unfortunately for Kodak, a company named Polaroid had already produced similar cameras and films and had taken out patents on various designs. Legal advisers assured Kodak that its products did not interfere with the Polaroid patents and that there was therefore nothing to worry about.

As soon as the Kodak instant cameras were released on the market, Polaroid sued Kodak claiming that some patents had been copied. After a legal battle that raged for ten years, Kodak was sorely disappointed when the courts supported Polaroid in its case.

Kodak immediately recalled all its instant cameras and compensated their owners. In 1991 Kodak was ordered to pay Polaroid $924.5 million.

The wisdom of varied products

Seeking a new product to take over where the Instamatic left off, Kodak produced disc cameras in 1982. Instead of using rolled film, these small cameras had tiny negatives held on a disc. The design and engineering of the system was brilliant, but the concept was flawed. In all, around twenty-five million disc cameras were sold before production was halted in 1988. To Kodak this was almost a failure – it had hoped that the disc system would be the most successful yet. The mainly Japanese competition stayed with the 35mm cameras. Perhaps for the first time, Kodak was not a market leader.

Although Kodak struggled to sell the quantities of cameras that it hoped for in the 1980s, the company still consistently made profits. One reason for this was its interests in profitable industries other than photography.

During the 1950s Tennessee Eastman had manufactured artificial thread for rugs and curtains and Texas Eastman synthesized chemicals from oil and gas. In the 1960s Carolina Eastman produced Kodel polyester for making clothes and ten years later the Arkansas Eastman Company had made organic chemicals.

By 1980, the year of Kodak's one hundredth anniversary, the company was producing a blood analyzer. In 1981, Kodak sales exceeded $10 billion, nearly 20% of which was for products unrelated to photography.

In the 1990s, Kodak was manufacturing laser

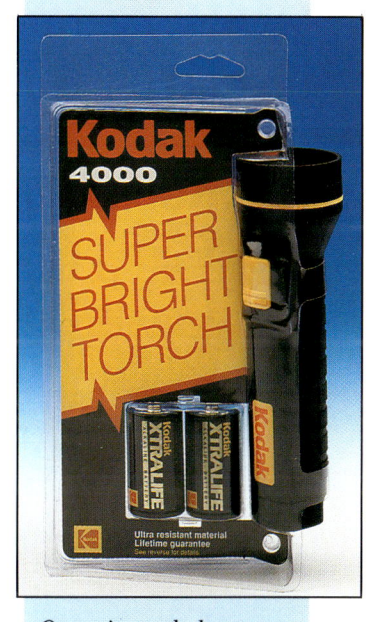

Opposite and above: By 1986 Kodak had branched out into batteries, with a variety of goods to accompany them. Soon videos, disposable cameras, and computer programs were also part of the product list. By the 1990s Kodak manufactured hundreds of products that had nothing or little to do with photography – it sold almost two thousand brands and trademarks in more than 150 countries. This wide product base meant that, if sales were low in one area, the profits of the company could be maintained in others.

printers, home improvement materials, photocopiers, and videotapes. It maintained its research departments as well – in 1993 alone, Kodak was granted 1,008 patents in the United States.

The future

In spite of all these different interests, Kodak will always be linked with photography, and the company has always been dedicated to researching new photographic products.

In recent years, Kodak has explored and developed a completely new photographic system –

Main picture: The Olympic games, such as the Seoul Olympics in 1988 pictured here, were a great photographic opportunity. For this reason, Kodak opted to be the official imaging sponsor of the 1994 Winter Olympics held in Lillehammer, in Norway.
Top: The fall of the Berlin wall, something once thought to be impossible, captured on Kodak film.
Bottom: An oil well on fire in the Middle East. An example of the possibilities of modern film.

As well as operating a research and development policy that perpetually aimed to improve camera and film quality, Kodak also pursued new ideas. In 1990 it launched a revolutionary photo-CD system in which images were transferred onto disc and then viewed on a television screen.

"George Eastman's lively and inventive mind, his gift for organization and management, and his instinctive feel for what the public wanted are still qualities fundamental to Kodak today."

From Kodak in the U.K., a Kodak publication.

the Photo Compact Disc. With this system, images are transferred onto a compact disc, from which they can be relayed onto a television screen or transmitted down a telephone line. It is a system that uses the innovative technology that Kodak continually researched so that it could stay ahead of the opposition.

By the mid-1990s, Kodak marketed two thousand Kodak products in more than 150 countries. However it still adhered to many of George Eastman's ideals and concepts. One of these concerns was caring for the environment. Kodak recycled products whenever possible. In keeping with this philosophy in 1990, it had introduced a family of fun cameras for single use only. These inexpensive cameras were sold complete with film and, when the film had been exposed, the camera was returned to a photofinisher. The photofinisher developed the film and returned the camera case to Kodak where it was recycled to make a new camera. It was a simple idea that was a huge success. In 1993, more than 100 million single-use cameras were sold. George Eastman would have approved.

Important Dates

1854	July 12: George Eastman is born to George Washington and Maria Kilbourn Eastman, in Waterville, New York, in the United States.
1868	George Eastman leaves school at the age of fourteen in order to take a job as a messenger boy for an insurance firm.
1874	Eastman takes a job as a junior clerk at the Rochester Savings Bank, earning $800 a year.
1878	Eastman becomes interested in wet-plate photography.
1879	Eastman continues to work on perfecting an emulsion recipe for making photographic dry plates. Later in the year he produces and patents a machine that coats plates with emulsion and makes mass production possible.
1880	April: Eastman goes into business manufacturing dry plates in Rochester, New York.
1881	Henry Strong goes into partnership with Eastman and the Eastman Dry Plate Company is formed. Sept.: With the growing success of his new company, Eastman leaves his job at the bank to devote more time to his new business.
1882	The Eastman Dry Plate Company experiences a problem with the gelatin on the plates and replaces all the faulty merchandise, establishing a reputation for quality and fairness.
1884	The Eastman Dry Plate and Film Company is created. Eastman negative paper is introduced but not released for sale until the following year.
1885	Eastman and camera maker William Walker invent the first roll holder for negative paper. Transparent American film is produced.
1888	June: Eastman conjures up the name Kodak for his new compact camera, which is promoted with the catchphrase, "You push the button – We do the rest."
1889	The Eastman Photographic Materials Company Limited is established in London, England. Aug.: The first commercial celluloid film is developed and marketed.
1891	Kodak Park is created in Rochester, New York, and a factory is built near London, in England. Thomas Edison invents the Kinetoscope – the forerunner of the modern movie camera – which heralds the arrival of the movie industry and a whole new market for film.
1892	Realizing that the name Kodak is at least as famous as his own, Eastman changes the company name to the Eastman Kodak Company.
1895	German physicist Wilhelm Roentgen discovers X-rays, highlighting another market for Eastman and Kodak. Frank Brownell develops the successful Folding Kodak and Pocket Kodak cameras.
1898	Eastman Photographic Materials in Britain and the Eastman Kodak Company of New York are joined into a single company, Kodak Limited.

1899	Eastman begins a profit-sharing scheme among his work force, which becomes known as the "divvy."
1900	Frank Brownell develops the hugely successful camera known as the Brownie, which is sold for just $1.
1904	Eastman cuts his employees working day from ten to nine hours, with no loss of pay.
1912	The "divvy", the Wage Dividend, is formalized into a profit-sharing scheme.
1913	Kodak's first commercial research laboratory, one of the first laboratories of its kind in the United States, is opened. Kodak faces legal battles over the patent of celluloid film.
1914	Kodak scientist John Capstaff develops a film named Kodachrome, which uses red and green.
1917	The first Eastman dental clinic is established in Rochester; in the years that follow, more such clinics are created in cities all over the world.
1919	Eastman's partner, Henry Strong, dies.
1921	U.S. courts rule against Kodak buying up any companies in the future to prevent the company from becoming a monopoly.
1923	Kodak releases the home movie camera, the Cine-Kodak Motion Picture Camera. Eastman hands over the running of the company to become chairman of the board of directors.
1928	Kodacolor film is first produced. Kodak enters education with the Eastman Teaching Films Corporation.
1930	The company Tennessee Eastman is founded. It eventually manufactures synthetic textiles – the first Kodak products not to be directly related to photography.
1932	March 14: George Eastman, aged seventy-seven, commits suicide at home after being ill for some years. He leaves his estate to the University of Rochester.
1935	Kodachrome – a film using red, green, and blue – is developed and sold commercially for the first time.
1949	Kodacolor film is finally released on the market.
1950	Kodak is awarded an Oscar for producing a safety film to replace the highly flammable cellulose nitrate film that was commonly used in the movie industry.
1963	The hugely popular Kodak Instamatic cameras are introduced – more than seventy million are sold.
1976	Kodak enters the instant camera market and soon runs into trouble with a rival company, Polaroid, which claims it already owns the patent on the instant camera design.
1991	Kodak is ordered to pay Polaroid $924.5 million in settlement of the patent battle.
1994	Kodak is ranked as one of the twenty-five largest U.S. companies, with manufacturing facilities in five continents and commercial outlets in more than 150 countries.

Glossary

Capital: The amount of surplus or disposable money that a *company* or individual has.

Cine camera: A camera that takes a series of still pictures – twenty-four photographs each second – which are then projected onto a screen one after another, giving the impression of movement.

Company: A group of two or more people that is registered to carry out a trade or business. A company is obliged to conform to certain regulations which may vary from country to country or from state to state in the U.S.

Company treasurer: An official in a *company* who is responsible for all the financial matters relating to the *company*.

Copyright: The exclusive right given, by law, to an inventor or writer to protect his or her invention or work from being copied for a certain period of time.

Developing: A process in photography in which a *film* or plate is treated with chemicals to produce a visible image.

Dividend: In business, the sum of money paid out of the *company profits* to *company* shareholders. It is usually paid out once or twice a year.

Entrepreneur: A person with a sharp commercial sense who sets up a new business and takes risks to make the business successful and profit-making.

Exposure: The number of individual pictures on a roll of *film*; or the time a piece of *film* needs to be exposed to the light in order to allow the image to form on the *film* properly.

Film or film base: A strong, flexible, and thin transparent strip that has been coated with *photographic emulsion*.

Gelatin: A natural substance obtained from bone and skin and other animal tissue. It is transparent, with no smell, and is used in the photographic process.

General manager: A person who is elected to organize and lead a *company*. He or she is responsible for making critical decisions that will help the *company* achieve its business goals.

Incorporated or public limited company: A *company* formed by several owners. Each owner is responsible, by law, for only a limited amount of the *company*'s debts.

Invest: To buy *shares* in a *company* in the hope that they will make a *profit*; or to buy an object, such as a house, that will increase in value and therefore make the buyer a *profit* when the object is eventually sold.

Market: In terms of a *company*'s sales plan, the number of people who might want to buy a particular product; it also means to sell the product in an organized and preplanned way.

Monopoly: The domination of one *company* over the selling of a particular product or service, or one particular *market*, to the extent that it is difficult for other *companies* to compete. This can mean that the dominant *company* is able to set its own price level and keep the price unreasonably high because it is the only business providing the product or service. There are laws against a *company* having a monopoly in this way.

Negative: The name given to the image formed on the photographic *film* after *exposure* and when the *film* has been developed. The tones of the image are reversed, with light areas appearing dark and dark areas appearing light.

Patent: The legal right granted to an inventor to exclusively make, use, and sell his or her invention for a limited time. To qualify for a patent the invention must be new and original. Once granted, no one can copy or use the invention without the express permission of the patent-holder.

Photographic emulsion: A light-sensitive layer with which photographic *film* is coated.

Positive: A positive print is made from a *negative* image, with the light areas returning to light and dark areas returning to dark.

Profit: The amount of money a *company* or individual has left over in a business venture after costs and expenses have been paid.

Share: An equal part of a *company*'s *capital* that can be bought and owned by a member of the *company* or public. If a person buys a share, he or she is then entitled to a percentage of the *company*'s *profits*.

Spool: A reel around which something, in this case photographic *film*, can be wound.

Stock market: The place where *shares* in different *companies* are bought and sold.

Transparency: An individual image on transparent *film*.

Index

American film 21, 24
Archer, Frederick Scott 12

Bromide paper 21-22
Brownell, Frank 31-32, 37
Brownie, The 37-38, 51, 56

Cameras,
  numbers sold 26, 33-34, 37-38, 56-7
  types of
    Brownie 37-38, 51, 56
    cine 47-48, **63**
    compact 22-24
    disc 57
    folding 32-33
    Instamatic 56-57
    movie 31
    pocket 32-33
    single-use 60
Capstaff, John 43
Coating, see Plates

Daguerre, Louis 12
Daguerrotype 12
Dry-plate photography 13-17, 19-20

Eastman, George
  birth of 10
  as businessman 5, 9, 14, 20, 49, 53
  death of 53
  as entrepreneur 9-10, 25-26, 47-48, **63**
  family of 10, 38
  first employment 12
  forms first company 15
  generosity of 42, 52-53
  illness 51
  inventor 9-10, 19, 22-24
  manager 20
  partnership with Henry Strong 15
  and patents 13-14, **63**
  and photography
    early interest in 5-6, 8-9
  retirement of 53
  schooldays 10
  Welfare of employees
    Accident, Benefits and Pensions Fund 38
    dividend 37, **63**
    profit sharing 37, 48-49, **63**
    working hours 38
Eastman Dry Plate Company 15-16
Eastman Dry Plate and Film Company 20
Eastman Kodak Company 10, 29, 35

Eastman Photographic Materials Company 27
Eastman Savings and Loan Association 48
Eastman Teaching Films Corporation 48
Edison, Thomas 31, 48
Emulsion, photographic 8-10, 13-14, 17, 19-21, 27, **63**

Film, **63**
  American 21, 24
  cartridge 56
  celluloid 27
  cine 31, **63**
  developing 24, **63**
  invention of 19-22
  Kodacolor 48
  negative 19-22, **63**
  paper 19
  roll 27
  transparency 27, **63**
  X-ray 43
Fox Talbot, William 12

Glass, plate 8-9, 16-17, 19-21
Goodwin, Rev. Hannibal 27, 43

Kinetoscope 31
Kodachrome 43, 54
Kodacolor 56
Kodak Ltd
  advertising 19-20 24-26, 46
  business strategy 19, 29
  distribution 29
  employees 36-38, 41, 48-49
  exports 19
  faulty products of 16-17
  future of 58, 60
  growth 16-17, 27, 29-31, 34, 36-37, 46
  legal disputes 27, 43, 45, 57
  marketing 17, 26, 29, **63**
  monopoly 34, 45, **63**
  name derivation of 23-24
  Oscar award 47
  other products 6, 46, 54-55, 57-58, 60
  patents 21, 27, 35, 43, 47, 56-57, **63**
  publicity 29, 55-56
  reputation of 17
  research 22, 41-3, 53-55, 58, 60
  sales 16, 30, 57
  slogan, advertising 24
  technology 60
  trademark of 23-24
Kodak Girl 25
Kodak Hour 51
Kodak Park 29, 42

Kodak Primer 24
Kodak projector 47
Kodaslide projector 54

Maddox, R.L. 13
Massachusetts Institute of Technology (M.I.T.) 42, 53

Negative 12, 16, 19-22, **63**
Niepce, Joseph 12

Photographic kit 6
Photography
  aerial 45
  of environment 60
  growth of 26-27, 29-31, 45-46, 54
  history of 6-7, 12-13
  instant 56
  processes used in
    bromide 21, **63**
    dry-plate 13-17, 19-20
    enlargement 22
    film 19, **63**
    glass plates 8-9, 16-17, 19-20
    negative 12, 19-22, **63**
    wet-plate 8-9, 12-13
  types of camera 12, 24, 31, 47, 54, 56-57, 60
  use of during wars 45, 54
Plates
  dry 13-17, 19-20
  glass 8-9, 16-17, 19-21
  machine coating of 14
  wet 8-9, 12-13
  X-ray 31
Polaroid 56-57
Positive 12, 19-22, **63**

Reichenbach, Henry 22, 27
Readymount 54
RDX 55
Roentgen, Wilhelm 31
Roll holder 20

Shares 35-37, 48, **63**
Strong, Henry 15, 34

Technicolor Corporation 47
Trademark 23-24
Translucene 20
Transparency 27, 56, **63**
Tennessee Eastman Company 46

Walker, William 20
Wet-plate photography 8-9, 12-13
Wratten and Wainwright 41

X-ray 31, 43

METROPOLITAN BOROUGH OF ST. HELENS
RAINHILL HIGH SCHOOL
WARRINGTON ROAD, RAINHILL,
MERSEYSIDE. Tel: 051-430 0070
LIBRARY

11283